Why I Quit Going to Church

Terry Austin

Why I Quit Going to Church
Terry Austin

Published by Austin Brothers Publishing, Fort Worth, Texas

www.abpbooks.com

ISBN 978-0-9996328-9-5

Copyright © 2018 by Terry Austin

ALL RIGHTS RESERVED. *No part of this book may be reproduced in any form without permission in writing from the publisher, except in the case of brief quotations embodied in critical reviews or articles.*

Printed in the United States of America

2018 -- First Edition

Dedicating this book to someone is an easy choice. Only one person has walked with me through all the experiences and lessons reflected on these pages.

My wife

Sharon

has patiently and tirelessly travelled the road with little complaint but with frequent challenges to make sure my heart is right.

Contents

Introduction	7
Why I Quit Going to Church	23
The Dissolution of Church Stewardship	37
Why Do You Give Money to Your Church?	45
Is That Building Really Necessary?	63
Why Do We Keep Setting Up Our Pastors to Fail?	77
When Churches Go Wrong	89
When the Church Chooses Country over Christ	111
Critical and Judgmental	133
American Christianity and Dementia	145
Conclusion	159

Dear Church Leader,

If you are interested in a potential church member, here I am. My wife and I are prime candidates to be a part of your congregation. We are ready to be welcomed and put to work.

Both of us are experienced and quite capable. We were both raised in families where church involvement was at the hub of family life, and the subject of most conversations around the dinner table. I have served as a pastor for more than 15 years, and a church consultant for nearly 20 years.

Yes, I know you can do the math–that puts us in our mid-60's. We might not fit the target demographic of your church, but I can assure you the problem is not with us. We don't especially want to be a part of a senior adult ministry, and I think I am correct in saying that younger folks are comfortable with us so our presence won't torpedo your ministry plans.

I will confess up front that you might want to accuse me of being too selective when it comes to church. I like to think it is because I have high standards. Either way, what I'm trying to say is I'm not interested in what you are doing simply because you tack the word "church" onto your legal papers.

For the past few years, I have felt like we were living on an island all by ourselves, but I recently discovered I actually belong to a labeled category of people. Church leaders have long talked about the "unchurched." Apparently, there is another group of people known as the "dechurched."

This term is used to describe those who have left the historic Christian faith. This group consists primarily of young people who grew weary of the church's message that if you obey God your life will be blessed. They dropped out of church once they saw the fallacy of this message and began to experience the natural pain and sorrow of life. They were once a part of the church, but because their experience didn't ring true with the church's message, they walked away.

However, that group doesn't accurately describe me either. I did not leave the church because of the message. In fact, I don't think I have ever left the church. The problem is that the church left me. I have always been there, still plugging away trying to do the work of Jesus, but the church wandered off doing something else.

The church has been extremely busy doing politics. Not the kind of politics I was taught from my youth when we were encouraged to pray for our leaders and respect those in authority, but the politics that require allegiance to a set of dogmas. I have discovered that unless I condone specific political positions, I will be treated like Cinderella by her stepsisters.

The church has also been about the task of judgmentalism. I was taught growing up that specific behaviors are wrong and should be avoided, but I was also taught that I was not the judge and jury of another. Consequently, our home and our church were open to whoever needed our hospitality. The stories of the woman caught in adultery, Jesus' overhearing the prayer of the Pharisee, the open embrace of Zacchaeus, and other episodes wrapped up in Jesus' words, "Judge not, lest you be judged" were planted deep within my conscience.

I remember the excitement buzzing through the congregation when the worst sinner in town would show up for a revival meeting. I recall preaching the funeral for a man in our community just six months after he stood in my living room threatening to beat me up even though he was unrepentant. I did my best to show mercy and compassion to his family. Now I find those who belonged to the same church with me standing on the street corner holding hateful signs and sharing disgusting Facebook posts. One of us has changed churches, and I don't think it was me.

The church also pulled away from me when it began to build fences rather than bridges. In fact, I wrote a book a few years back with the subtitle, "Building a Church Without Fences." I'm not a fan of fences, yet it seems the church is in favor of them, whether it is along the Rio

Grande border, a stigma given to those of other faiths, or an invisible barrier to separate those who don't look like us.

The church also left me when the decision was made to become an entertainment venue, committed to competing with the best the world has to offer. I grew up with the understanding that most people did not attend on Sunday night because we could not compete with Walt Disney Presents on television. I don't need the church to entertain me; I get cable. That is not the purpose of the church, but somehow the quest to offer the best has choked out the necessity of making disciples.

My complaint is not about the music or worship styles, but about the substance of the church. The church, by definition, is unique, unlike anything else in the world. The church consists of followers of Jesus, those occasionally described in scripture as the poor and outcast, those who are not wise, wealthy, or powerful (see 1 Corinthians 1:26). If you seek those who will make your congregation powerful and influential, then leave me alone.

But, if you are the leader of a church who wants a passionate follower of Christ, a careful student of the Bible, an experienced practitioner of the faith taught by Jesus, I'm available. But let me give you a head's up: don't come knocking on my door hoping that I will join your crusade to build a politically involved powerful organization that is striving to establish the kingdom of God in this place. All

I want is a group of fellow followers of Jesus who want to be faithful to Him.

Sincerely,
Terry Austin

Introduction

If you want to write and publish a book, the most fundamental question you must answer is, "Who is going to read this book?"

I've worked with many writers over the years, and the first answer they typically give is that the book is for everyone. That's understandable because if we take the time to write a book, the subject must be vital to us. Therefore, it must be relevant to everyone.

Alas, that's not the case. Not everyone reads every book.

I've also learned that it doesn't even need to be a good book to attract a lot of readers. Good writing helps, of course, but people are drawn to a subject. Poor writing might turn them away, but it was the subject matter that attracted them to the book in the first place.

So, I asked the question when I began writing this book—who is going to read this book?

A while back, I posted an article on my blog that I titled, "Why I Quit Going to Church." I thought it was a good article, but to be honest, I think that every article I post is good. However, I've been a writer long enough to know that there's no predicting how readers will evaluate something.

I checked the statistics a few days after posting the article and noticed the article was being read by a large number of people. That's always a good feeling. Then I saw that it was frequently shared on Facebook. This continued for several weeks, and the number of readers of my blog grew exponentially.

After things slowed down, there were a couple of times when the article was floating around Facebook again. This happened off and on for about a year. The last time I checked, the article had been read by more than 50,000 people.

Apparently, I struck a nerve.

About the same time, I came across a Facebook page for a group of people who referred to themselves as "Unchurching." They were built around the publication of a book with the same name.

As I researched this group, I discovered some kindred folks. Up until then, I thought that I was the only one who felt this way about the church. Apparently, there are millions of others like me—folks who have simply stopped going to church.

I'm not talking about people who have turned their back on the Christian faith, or that ever-present group of people who got mad at someone or something and quit attending. We are people who are deeply involved with living a life of faith but have given up on being able to do that through the institutional church as it now exists in America.

I have been involved with church work my entire life, which has turned out to be quite a long time. There are times when I think I have seen just about everything there is to see about the church. One time I heard a preacher sing his entire sermon, every word, like a Broadway musical, only not very good singing. I have seen people fall in the baptistery, trip and stumble while entering the choir loft, and just about every other kind of pratfall you can imagine. I have been served Gold Fish and chicken noodle soup for communion and eaten unidentifiable stuff at a church supper. If I really tax my memory, I could make a list several pages long of unusual things I have witnessed at church.

Several years ago I heard about a stunt involving a pastor and a bed on the church roof that opened my eyes to something horrible that was happening with the church (I'll explain it in detail in a later chapter). Learning about that stunt that generated nationwide publicity, caused me to begin thinking seriously about what the church had become.

Prior to quitting church, we spent a great deal of time looking around—or "church shopping" as it's often called. We found ourselves in a variety of churches for a variety of reasons. I recall one that we had no interest in joining, and it's part of a denomination that doesn't interest me.

However, it's in our neighborhood, although kind of off the beaten path. We don't know anyone who attends, but at 11 o'clock on a Sunday morning, we found ourselves sitting in the sanctuary prepared for worship.

Before the beginning of the service, there was a great deal of bustle and commotion. The small ten-piece orchestra and twelve voice choir were putting the final touches on the music for the day. We were handed a bulletin upon entering and made our way to a pew about a third of the way down the middle aisle.

Other than the gentleman who handed me the bulletin in the foyer no one spoke a word to us. Several folks were standing outside the front door, a small group in the lobby, and some individuals milling about the sanctuary, but not a word of introduction or greeting. The pastor, already dressed in his robe, walked past me twice without as much as a nod.

I wasn't sure if there was a problem. I had brushed my teeth and put on clean clothes earlier in the morning. My hair was combed, and I even shaved (something that I don't always do). I don't have any piercings or tattoos that some might find off-putting. As I looked around it was apparent that Sharon and I fit neatly within the demographic that currently attend the church.

Perhaps it was the wheelchair. I have discovered that many are uncomfortable around a person in a wheelchair. However, they will usually say "hello" or something else trite, even if they don't want a conversation. But, in this church on this Sunday morning, not a word.

The service began with a solid ten minutes of announcements. I know God must have been blessed and all of us felt prepared to worship after that–just kidding!

Yet, it was something said during the announcements that caught my attention and became the most memorable part of this experience. The church is planning a giant pumpkin patch in the next couple of weeks. They put out the call for help to unload the truck full of orange melons.

Certainly fall is just around the corner, complete with Halloween and Thanksgiving, so there is a need for pumpkins. The church has an ample open space next to the parking lot–the perfect place for a pumpkin patch. I'm not sure that anyone would have a problem with the church providing the community with a place to secure their pumpkin needs for the holidays.

The woman making the announcement was quick to explain that the purpose was to introduce the church to the neighborhood and have the opportunity to meet and invite people to attend church. It makes sense. They want to meet new people and encourage them to become a part of their church.

But, there we were, new people to the church and not a single person welcomed us, encouraged us, or invited us to get involved. They did not ask for our name, help us find a place to sit, tell us about themselves, or even acknowledge our existence. It seemed odd that they were planning to spend hundreds of dollars and invest countless hours in an activity that would allow them to do precisely what they were failing to do already.

I wonder if churches are so busy trying to do big things that they miss the simple opportunities right in front of them. Many churches will probably begin preparations for their Christmas extravaganza soon, hoping to lure the community to come visit their church. However, they might be too busy to take the time to walk across the street and get to know the people that live in the neighborhood.

It was an unintended message, but what I heard from the church that Sunday was if you want to really feel welcome here, come and buy one of our pumpkins. Hopefully, they will carve a few happy, welcoming faces on those pumpkins before they sell them.

Our adventure to find a church continued to a Lutheran church. We were giving everyone a fair shot and also found ourselves at Catholic, Methodist, Assembly of God, Presbyterian, Independent, non-Denominational (although not sure the difference between those last two) and of course Baptist churches. In fact, this was the second Lutheran church for us.

The first was somewhat unusual. It is the closest Lutheran congregation to our house, just a few blocks up the street. Although I have studied a great deal about Martin Luther in college and seminary, I knew little of the Lutheran church today. I expected to encounter a formal, liturgical style of worship, which is something I typically enjoy.

However, this particular Lutheran church was no different than any other church we have visited that is enamored with what is known as contemporary worship. It began with the first beat of the worship team. The bass was so loud and the pounding so vibrantly that Sharon almost had to leave.

The most unusual thing that morning was the announcement that the men's Bible study group would be meeting next week at a nearby brewery. If you attend and pay the twenty-dollar entrance fee, you will not only be able to participate in Bible study, you will also receive two pints of their finest brew. That part does sound like something Martin Luther might have enjoyed, but it is not something I have ever encountered in church before.

But the Lutheran church I want to describe was nothing like that. It was extremely liturgical, which I had deduced from their website, and I was looking forward to the experience. Although the liturgy was a little different than what I expected, that was not the most noticeable thing about our church experience.

One of the first (and last) folks to speak to us was a pleasant gentleman standing just outside the door leading into the sanctuary. He asked if we were visitors. I don't know for sure, but I suspect he already knew the answer to that question. When I confirmed his suspicion, he didn't introduce himself or ask anything about us. He just handed us a card and said we would need this. That was the unusual part because unlike what I anticipated, it was not a visitor's card requesting a name and contact information.

The purpose of the card was "Registration for Holy Communion." It read as follows: "Attendance at the Lord's Table is limited to communicant members of _____ Lutheran Church and to visitors from Lutheran congregations in altar and pulpit fellowship with us. If you have not communed in the past six months, please speak to the Pastor before communing at this altar."

This statement was followed by an admonition from the Apostle Paul to examine myself in several different categories. Finally, it provided a place to date and sign the card and a note to update my address on the back of the card.

I'll be honest. I read this card before the worship service started and it didn't sit well with me. In fact, we didn't make it to the end when they had communion, choosing

Why I Quit Going to Church

instead to make our way to the exit during the collection of the offering.

Essentially this church was saying to me, a visitor, that I'm not welcome at the Lord's Table. By not participating, according to the card, I was declaring that I'm not a believer, or I'm not a Lutheran, or I have wandered away from the faith for at least six months.

My problem is that I'm not sure the Lord's Table was established for that purpose. Now don't misunderstand, this is not something new to me. I've been around the block, so to speak, when it comes to churches. My father was a Baptist preacher out of the Landmark tradition (look it up), and he believed that only members of the local church should take the Lord's Supper. He believed that, but he would have never told a visitor that they couldn't participate. He would have never let it be a stumbling block.

In addition, I have even preached at a church on a Sunday when they were sharing the Lord's Supper, and since I was the "visiting preacher" I was not invited to participate.

But that's not right. I do not understand how folks have come up with the notion that the purpose of communion (Lord's Supper, Lord's Table, whatever you want to call it) is to make a declaration of faith and church membership. That is the purpose of baptism.

When I was the pastor of a small church, one of our regular attendees came to my office during the week before we had a Lord's Supper scheduled for the next Sunday. He volunteered to sit in the back on Sunday morning and point out people who should not be included. I'm not sure what he had in mind and how that would happen, but I firmly rejected his gracious offer.

When Jesus instituted the Supper, he even included Judas in the meal, even though he already knew Judas wasn't with him. What I see is perhaps a final plea for Judas to recognize that Jesus really is the source of life and sustenance; one more effort to keep him from carrying out his plan of betrayal.

Why would we not invite everyone to participate? It is the Lord's Table. How dare we presume to tell someone else they are not worthy. I'm not worthy—neither are you.

The only thing Sharon and I heard from this particular Lutheran church is that we are not qualified to share at the Lord's Table. Why would we ever want to become a part of that fellowship?

Communion has provided some of the most memorable worship experiences in my life. It is an awe inducing-privilege to be invited to share the meal that Jesus instituted and to share it with others who are also seeking to make their way through life. I would even go so far as to suggest that rather than being a means of identifying who is in and who is out, it is an evangelistic opportunity (think about it).

This Lutheran church was different in many ways than most of the churches we visited. By throwing up a barrier to belong to their congregation, they are the exact opposite of what the majority of churches are doing today. To be honest, in visiting a number of churches from a variety of denominations, it impossible to tell them apart. There is very little difference in churches.

A great deal of effort is being invested in growing large churches. Growing up and being educated and trained as a Southern Baptist, I have worshipped around the altar of church growth for a long time. Everything is about increasing the size of the church, getting more people to "join the church" and come to the Sunday morning services. I have been a pastor and felt the pressure of reporting good attendance numbers week after week. Many ministry failures can be excused as long as the average attendance increases year after year.

As a child, I was encouraged to memorize "The Great Commission" at the end of Matthew's Gospel where Jesus instructed his followers to go out and grow the church. If there was ever a concern about focusing too much on numbers we were told that it is biblical–the Book of Acts records three thousand being saved in one day and there is an entire book of the Old Testament with the name Numbers.

When I was the pastor of a very rural church with virtually no possibility of increased membership numbers, I struggled with thinking I was doing something wrong. Perhaps I was not working hard enough, or maybe I just was not the pastor this community needed. Back in those days, the Southern Baptist Convention gave an award to the "Small Church Pastor of the Year." However, it was always given to a pastor who had turned a small church into a large church.

It now seems that some folks have figured out how to do this and they are growing churches into the thousands and ten thousand. In the Dallas/Fort Worth Metroplex where I live numerous churches have more than a thousand attend every week. They can be found in every nook and cranny of the city. Perhaps a half a dozen or more of these churches report more than ten thousand in attendance. Church growth has been a success!

Or has it?

I have studied the New Testament for many years and have come to the conclusion that the work of the church is not about enormous growth. Especially when you consider the ministry of Jesus, there is little concern about accumulating large numbers of followers. In fact, it sounds like Jesus almost made it impossible for large numbers of people to follow him. Listen to these verses:

"Enter through the narrow gate; for the gate is wide and the way is broad that leads to destruction, and there are many who enter through it. For the gate is small and the way is narrow that leads to life, and there are few who find it." Matthew 7:13-14

"And he who does not take his cross and follow after Me is not worthy of Me. He who has found his life will lose it, and he who has lost his life for My sake will find it." Matthew 10:38-39

Then Jesus said to His disciples, "If anyone wishes to come after Me, he must deny himself, and take up his cross and follow Me. For whoever wishes to save his life will lose it; but whoever loses his life for My sake will find it." Matthew 16:24-25

These verses are just a sample of many of the things Jesus did that would discourage and drive away a crowd.

Perhaps these words of Jesus suggest that those who have been successful at growing a large congregation might have done so at the cost of changing the message. There is no mass appeal in Jesus' words. I'm not saying that God cannot or will not bring together a large group of people. It happened in the book of Acts, and it has happened a few times in history since. However, it is indeed not the norm, and I would not expect to find hundreds of these unusual congregations in north Texas.

There was an interesting testimony about this matter in Leadership Journal a few years ago. Walter Kallestad was pastor of a two-hundred-member church in Phoenix. While standing in line to purchase tickets for a movie he had an epiphany. "The only way to capture people's attention is entertainment, I thought. If I want people to listen to my message, I've got to present it in a way that grabs their attention long enough for me to communicate the gospel."

Not surprisingly, it worked. "For us, worship was a show, and we played to a packed house. We grew by thousands, bought more land, and positioned ourselves to reach even more people. Not that any of this is wrong in and of itself - people coming to faith in Christ isn't bad. I told myself it was good - I told others it was good… By the time we service the $12-million debt, pay the staff, and maintain the property, we've spent more than a million before we can spend a dime on our mission. At the time, we had plans for a spectacular worship center with a retractable roof."

After some serious soul-searching, time in prayer, and study of what God was doing with other congregations, Kallestad came to this conclusion: "We were entertaining people as a substitute for leading them into the presence of God."

This church made an immediate change from entertainment to learning how to enter into true worship of God and relationships with one another. People responded in the same way they responded to Jesus–they left. However, as the church changed something even more significant happened. "I used to ask, 'What can we do to get more people to attend our church?' Now I ask, 'How can I best equip and empower the people to go be the church in the marketplace where God has called them to serve?'"

This is real church growth. Not necessarily numerical growth but growth toward becoming more like Jesus. It will probably never be an especially popular type of increase because it cannot be measured so we cannot take credit for it. Jesus' message is hard. Although His miraculous works attracted large crowds, his message scattered them quickly.

I think true church growth should be less about attracting large crowds to come and "be blessed" by our great music, awesome programs, and attractive facilities and more about sending followers of Jesus into the world to bless others. It is time to move away from the model of growth that we have adopted from the business world and return to a model of growth that focuses on spiritual depth and relationship.

All of our experiences with the many different churches stirred my dissatisfaction with the church. Allow me to clarify something before I go any further. When I use the term "church" in this context, I'm speaking about the institutional church. It is primarily the American church because I don't know anything about other countries.

I'm still a firm believer in the church that Jesus' established and promised would prevail against the "gates of hell." In fact, I could never quit going to that church because I am an integral part of that church. I believe the church consists of the followers of Christ.

However, the institutional church as it exists in America today is a far cry from the church Jesus founded. That sounds harsh, I know, but don't take it personally until you listen to my argument. If you stick with me through the pages of this book, I think many of you will find yourself in agreement.

Let me quickly add that I'm not advocating that anyone quit church—that's between you and God. I'm merely sharing my experience and my rationale in the hope that Christians will find a way to do church that is consistent with what is taught and exemplified in the New Testament.

Why I Quit Going to Church

As I indicated in the introduction, Sharon and I have visited numerous churches in the past few years. We counted one time and realized we have been to at least two each of Lutheran, Presbyterian, Methodist, Assembly of God, Catholic, and non-denominational, in addition to countless Baptist churches. However, for the last two years, more often than not, most weeks find us not attending any church.

It is correct to say that we have quit going to church.

To be honest, I never thought I would make such a statement. I have been in church from the beginning.

Somewhere in the Bible, it says, "In the beginning, God created church and Terry was there."

My father was a pastor, so our family life was centered on church. As I grew up, unlike many "preacher's kids," I never rebelled and left the church. I stayed with it—through high school, college, and my earliest working days. When I returned to college a few years later, it was to prepare for the ministry. It was time for me to become the preacher.

After seminary, I almost quit church. No church was interested in me being their pastor, and I was discouraged. After a short time, I was discovered and put back to work, and once again the church was the center of my world.

Not true any longer.

Although I quit going to church, my relationship with Jesus is as strong as ever. I still pray, read the Bible, study scripture, share my faith, and jump on opportunities for ministry as much as ever. My level of trust in God, dependence upon God, and recognition of God's presence has not waned.

When this first started happening, I thought there was something wrong with me. Even though I did not feel guilty for staying home on Sunday, I thought I should—at least a little guilt. But I didn't. I didn't think I was doing anything wrong. I thought that at least I must be a rare person—an active church member who drops out and doesn't feel guilty.

However, I came to realize that I am not rare. There are many of us, perhaps even millions of us. I have found a bunch who have traveled a similar path and ended up at the same location. These are people who love Jesus, who have been church leaders or active members and have quit the church.

The real question is why. Why did this happen? Why did I quit going to church?

I have given this much thought, and you will hear my answer. However, let me say a couple of things. First, you might feel like I am attacking you or something that is important to you. Let me assure you that is not my intention. As far as I'm concerned, you can continue attending church until Jesus returns and I will not try to change your mind.

Second, don't feel sorry for me. If you want to judge me, that's your business, but I don't need or want your sympathy. I'm a big boy, and I made a conscious decision after much thought and prayer. I don't need your approval or your condemnation.

Now, let me try and explain why I quit going to church.

I spent nearly 15 years, during the prime of my life, helping churches raise money. I wrote books and study material that was used by hundreds of thousands of people. I helped develop a capital fundraising program for buildings that has been utilized in thousands of churches. It is not an exaggeration to say that I have had a hand in raising more than a quarter of a billion dollars for churches.

You might think my ego is a little inflated, but it's not. I was good at what I did. However, now I think I was mistaken. I began to rethink the subject of money several years ago, and in 2010 I wrote a book titled, "Authentic Stewardship" to express the beginning of my change of thought. My journey continued, and in 2014 I wrote a blog post called, "The Dissolution of Christian Stewardship." It was seen as an attack on Dave Ramsey (although it wasn't), and people went nuts with thousands of readers daily for a long time, and then rediscovered and revived for some reason a year later.

In September of 2010, a friend and I started Bread Fellowship, a different kind of church built around the idea of keeping Christ in the center without a circumference. In other words, we would hold up Jesus as the central message and allow anyone to come and participate. I tried to capture this concept in a book I published in the summer of 2012. It is a great model that I still think has merit; however, it didn't work for me at that time.

Another significant experience along the way was a sermon I preached at Truett Theological Seminary in 2011. I was asked to address the subject of stewardship, which I did, but with a twist. Since it was a gathering of seminary students, aspirants for the church pulpit, I challenged them to think about the necessity to take a preaching position even if there was no salary. In other words, to consider working for Jesus without being paid.

It took me a long time to come to that position. In fact, I had to get to the point where I was making a living without depending on the church before I could see the value in not expecting the church to be my provider. I then began to realize that the church is better off without "paying the preacher." It sets everyone free to follow God's leadership.

Perhaps a more thorough explanation will be helpful before moving on. A pastor lives in the constant tension of pleasing enough of the right people to keep his job. Being a pastor is exactly like working for any business—you have a boss, and you must make the boss happy. This is even more complex because a pastor will probably have multiple bosses within the church. The problem for the pastor in that situation is that he is no longer serving Jesus. He is now serving the men and women who make up the local church (who may or may not be faithful servants of Jesus).

All of this is compounded by the fact that these same people who pay staff salaries are also the ones who must pay for the church building. Therefore, it is imperative to keep them happy, to make sure their needs are met, and that they bring in additional people for fresh sources of revenue.

I learned all of this while doing stewardship. If I were starting over today, I would not spend my most valuable years of ministry helping churches raise money. It has taken a long time, but I'm finally leaving all of that behind.

In fact, money is probably the reason I quit going to church. I don't mean the cost of attending, nor was I offended by being asked to give an offering. If churches are going to operate and be funded the way they are then asking for an offering is appropriate.

Before I expound on my understanding of the church, let me ask a question. If money were eliminated entirely from the equation, what would your church look like? In other words, if your church had no money what would happen? Would the church cease to exist? Or, would they find a way to do things without money?

While you ponder that question, I will share my opinion of the church today.

I am convinced the church in America today has become distracted from its purpose and focused on numbers rather than being the Body of Christ in the world. This has resulted in an overabundance of buildings and a failed understanding of the clergy. This is evidenced by the fact that the majority of the church's budget is consumed by the cost of construction and maintaining buildings, and paying staff salaries—as much as 80% of most instances.

Consequently, the church has created a self-perpetuating cycle that begins with the idea that a church must have a building. In order to afford the expense, enough people must join the local congregation and be encouraged to give money. To continually recruit new members additional staff members are necessary, who also cost money.

The consequences of this failure by the church are significant and include the following:

- Providing more and more expensive amenities to attract and keep people.
- Attempts to become full-service providers for people, offering everything folks need for entertainment, child care, youth activities, support groups, recreation, etc.
- Developing "worship services" that resemble musical concerts, complete with lights, video, and even pyrotechnics.
- Recruiting "worship leaders" who are essentially performers, and providing "worship services" that have little to do with New Testament worship.
- Churches with more than half of the registered members who are disconnected from the church and have little or no interest in following Jesus.
- Preachers who are unwilling or afraid to be prophetic because the church cannot afford to alienate significant members.
- A vast majority of believers who are not in a position to utilize their spiritual gifts because either they are not assigned a position by the church or because they don't have the gifts required for open positions at church.

- Churches have made a man (i.e., Senior Pastor) the head of the church rather than Christ. Or, perhaps they operate with a Board of Directors (Elders or Deacons), but not Christ.
- Pastors are under the burden of generating enough money to pay their salary and all the church financial obligations.
- Little money is available for helping the poor and needy.

Your church probably doesn't possess all these qualities, but even one of them is an indication that you are heading in the wrong direction. Also, this list doesn't even take into consideration the role politics has come to play in the life of the church—that's an entirely separate issue for another day.

Imagine how many poor people could have been helped, hungry people fed, orphans united with eager parents, or healing brought to the sick if that quarter of a billion dollars I helped raise would have been invested in something other than buildings and payrolls. But, money isn't the issue. The point is that the institutional church has ceased being the body of Christ in the world. Instead, it has become a self-perpetuating institution that sells physical comfort and spiritual assurance.

That last statement sounds rather harsh so trust me when I say it is not presented with a flippant attitude. Let me hasten to add that nothing I write here is intended to be a criticism of any individual. The finest Christians I know have given their life to serve the church. They are sincere and completely committed to serving Christ. However, like me, they have given their life to serving a church that is far off course.

If you are traveling and set a course that is merely one degree off target, it doesn't sound like such a big deal. In fact, after 100 yards you will be only five feet off. Two quick steps and you are back where you belong. However, after traveling one mile, you will be more than 90 feet off, and if you are going from San Francisco to Los Angeles, you will be off by six miles. The longer the trip the further away from the target that one simple degree will take you. If you travel around the world, you will be more than 430 miles off target.

The church in the New Testament set off in the direction established by the Holy Spirit. However, at some point, it was distracted just a little bit (about one degree). Now, 2,000 years later, the church is so far away from where it intended to go that the destination cannot even be seen on the horizon.

Church history tells us that there have been times when the deviation has been greater than one degree and other times when the church moved closer to the correct course. For example, Constantine and his attempts to make Christianity the official religion of the Roman world led us on a path that eventually went way offline. The Reformation and various spiritual awakenings have brought us back closer to the correct way. However, the end result is that the church in America today is nowhere near where it should be.

The result is an institution that is so encumbered with maintaining buildings, financially supporting staff, and striving to create a Christian world that it no longer has the will, energy, or desire to serve Jesus.

In order to correct this situation, I want to suggest a refocus on two essential doctrines of the Christian faith that can get us back on track. The first is the concept that the followers of Jesus make up the Body of Christ—the church. In other words, the church is not a place or a building—it is people. We are Christ's body in the world. The church is wherever we happen to be.

When two or more of us get together, then we have a gathering of the church. Since I have been in church my entire life, I have a good idea of what happens when the church gathers. There is singing, preaching, praying, announcing, plus entertaining, marketing and promotion, and a few other incidental activities. However, when I read scripture, I discover a different list of activities.

The second essential doctrine is the priesthood of all believers. Protestants have wrapped themselves in pride that they did away with the priesthood because of their belief that all of us are priests before God. However, they have substituted pastors for priests. The pastor today is viewed as a necessity in order to have a church, and many of them operate as if they have special access to God.

The American church has named the pastor as the CEO of the local church. It is the pastor who casts the vision, develops the plans, secures the resources, and sets the course for action. It is the pastor who explains God's word, leads the prayers, and finds the answers to people's problems.

In most churches, if you want to do something you are told to "ask the pastor" (or one of his staff representatives). If you have a message to share with the congregation the pastor will want to know about it beforehand (at least I would have when I was the pastor). If you desire to follow Christ in baptism, you need to talk to the pastor. If you want to renew your commitment of faith, then you go to the pastor.

In making the pastor the head of the church, we have placed him/her in an impossible situation—expecting them to do what only Christ can (and should) do. If we remove the pastor from the position of intermediary between Christ and the church, then everyone is allowed to function in direct relationship with Him. That is what the doctrine of the priesthood of all believers is about.

Now, let me return to my question—what would happen to the church if we remove money from the equation? In other words, the church does not have money for buildings, staff, or programs.

The first and most obvious thing is that Christians would gather in much smaller groups because the gathering would have to take place in homes, parks, and other public places. Imagine the dramatic change in the church if we eliminate the Sunday morning show along with the children's and young people's entertainment.

The next thing we would notice is that regular people would have to step up and do the work of the church since there is no longer a paid staff. The truth is that the ordinary people are to be doing the work of the church anyway. God has gifted each of us for service and ministry. He never expected that a pastor would be in charge of the church's work.

That raises another important point—the work of the church should take place out in the world, not within the walls of a church building. We gather to be encouraged and strengthened, and then we scatter to be the body of Christ in the world. We take the church with us because we are the church.

Imagine all of that—a small group of believers gathering in a home for the purpose of sharing and encouraging one another in the faith. By the way, I'm not making that up. Listen to these words:

Let us hold fast the confession of our hope without wavering, for He who promised is faithful; and let us consider how to stimulate one another to love and good deeds, not forsaking our own assembling together, as is the habit of some, but encouraging one another; and all the more as you see the day drawing near. (Hebrews 10:23-25)

This is not an admonition to gather in a large auditorium on Sunday morning as many want to suggest. Instead, it is a call not to try to live the Christian life in isolation—we do not have a Lone Ranger faith. We cannot make it on our own; we need one another. We are to gather with other believers to stimulate and encourage one another.

But it is not an admonition to gather and watch others and be entertained. When the church gathers there is to be sharing (including a meal, prayer needs/concerns, possessions with those in need—not an offering for the church, and the Lord's Supper). There is also to be encouraging one another (includes teaching, prayer, and spoken words). Finally, there should be praise, which includes singing and testimonies.

I have many believers in my life who share and encourage. Sharon and I strive to gather with others who desire to follow the leadership of Christ and help us be better representatives of Christ in the world. This is not an attempt to start a new church. It is merely a gathering of a minuscule portion of God's church.

When I say that I have quit going to church, what I really mean is that I have stopped going to what most people call the church. The truth is that I cannot quit because I am the church. I am the body of Christ in a unique corner of the world—the one I occupy. As a follower of Christ, you are also the church. When we get together, then we can have church, even if it's not in a building with a church sign in the yard.

The Dissolution of Church Stewardship

I stumbled into Christian Stewardship quite by accident. It was not on my list of interests or career choices, but as you know yourself, following God is not like mapping out the shortest route on your GPS. I have never been the smartest guy around, but I do know how to learn, so I set out to learn about stewardship.

As a child, I learned to tithe from my father. It was never a legalistic type of thing where you have to give a tenth or else God will be mad. It was just something we did. I never gave it much thought – until I found myself (as I said, quite by accident) working as a stewardship professional. In fact, I even received an award (complete with a very nice plaque) as the "Stewardship Professional of the Year." I am a good learner.

The stewardship thing worked out well for me and for a time I was one of the leading stewardship folks in the country. I have written material that has been used in thousands of churches around the world. There was a period of time when every stewardship item in the Southern Baptist world had my fingerprint on it somewhere.

There have been a couple of significant changes to stewardship during my lifetime. When I was a child, it was quite common to believe in tithing. However, during my teenage years, there was a movement to change that position. People began to teach that tithing is legalistic, and it is much more consistent with Jesus to be generous without specific guidelines. Tithing fell out of favor with many.

I remember well my introduction into this new world. It was at a small gathering of stewardship folks. I had already had a part in developing some material encouraging folks to be tithers. One of the men at this gathering was Cecil Ray, known by many Southern Baptists as the father of Baptist stewardship. I didn't know him personally, but I was well aware of his reputation.

Early in the meeting, Dr. Ray referred to those who taught tithing as "legalists." Out of respect and deference, I kept my mouth shut. (If you know me personally you probably don't believe that last statement.) During a break in the meeting, I told my supervisor if that old man calls me a legalist one more time we are going after it. He advised patience and keeping quiet.

I had the privilege of working with Dr. Ray several years later, after he retired, helping his church raise money in a building campaign. He was very gracious, even complimentary after I preached a sermon on tithing. I will hasten to say that even though he was not an advocate of tithing, I'm not sure I have ever met a more generous man. He gave significantly more than ten percent to his church.

However, this article is not about the tithe. The subject concerns another cosmic shift in stewardship teaching by the church; one that will have a devastating effect.

About halfway through my time of working in stewardship, there was a new interest in teaching money management. Church leaders concluded that one of the reasons people did not give generously to the church was because the desperate condition of their finances made it impossible. I saw the value of this approach and joined the parade by adding a financial management component to our material.

It got out of control. It got to the point that churches were only interested in teaching people how to handle their finances. Christian programs consisted of little more than quoting a few Bible verses in between guidelines for spending, saving, investing, and budgeting. The logical next step was to focus on getting out of debt – trusting that once people were out of debt, they would be generous givers.

Along came Dave Ramsey. Perhaps his biggest strength is the ability to make money. He took the "get out of debt" mantra to new heights, found a way to make money from helping folks get out of debt, and took the church stewardship world by storm. Churches quickly abandoned traditional stewardship teaching in favor of "Financial Peace."

I stumbled across an example of how extreme this approach became during my last year of leading church stewardship. A church, wanting to raise several million dollars for new construction, decided to forego traditional appeals to giving. Instead, they enrolled 500 families in Ramsey's course. Their rationale was that they would save the cost of fund-raising activities and consultation and when these families got out of debt, they would give generously to the building program. They were excited that Ramsey himself was going to come and speak to their congregation.

Genius for Ramsey; not so well thought out by the church. Ramsey would make about $50,000 selling material and for a one-time sermon. My experience with fund-raising is that the folks who are going to make a multi-million-dollar campaign successful are not in debt (at least, not consumer debt). Another thing I learned over the years is that getting out of debt does not make people generous givers.

The real problem is that Christians have anointed Ramsey as the stewardship sage and radically redefined stewardship teaching as good money management, or more narrowly as getting out of debt. The result is that we have made Dave Ramsey wealthy and robbed the church of an important doctrine – stewardship. It is probably accurate to say that the vast majority of churches that deliberately teach stewardship do it through a Dave Ramsey course.

Historically, biblical stewardship has led the church to take positions that are no longer considered to be Christian positions:

- Environment – stewardship education used to teach the value of taking care of the earth. Now, most evangelical Christians stand in opposition to environmental initiatives under the guise that they might harm the economy.
- Accumulation – for centuries the church taught the danger of having too much. Now, the emphasis seems to be on accumulating more and more because it is good for the economy.
- Responsibility – taking care of one another has always been a Christian focus. Now, many Christians complain about those who don't or can't take care of themselves and voice strong opposition to welfare and healthcare programs that give help to others.

When the leaders of a church stewardship movement become wealthy something is wrong. If there is any area of church ministry that should stand firm against wealth it should be stewardship.

"Keep deception and lies far from me, Give me neither poverty nor riches; Feed me with the food that is my portion, that I not be full and deny You and say, "Who is the LORD?" Or That I not be in want and steal, And profane the name of my God" (Proverbs 30:7-8).

"And Jesus said to His disciples, 'Truly I say to you, it is hard for a rich man to enter the kingdom of heaven. Again I say to you, it is easier for a camel to go through the eye of a needle, than for a rich man to enter the kingdom of God'" (Matthew 19:23-24).

It is a much too common problem with anyone in church leadership. If they are truly well-received, they are then confronted with the temptations of money and fame. It is hard to say "no" to either one of these opportunities. We love to turn our leaders into celebrities. When that happens, the focus is diverted to the leader and not Jesus.

It may be true (I don't know) that churches have more money than ever and that Christian families are leading the march in financial planning. However, it doesn't matter. That is not what stewardship is all about. Stewardship is not about wealth and accumulation. Church stewardship is not about large buildings and generous payrolls. Christian stewardship is learning to live with an open hand, not hanging onto the things of the world, but releasing them to be used by God and others.

Christian stewardship has very little to do with developing successful consumers. It is not the task of the church to teach people how to operate successfully in the world, but rather how to live successfully in a kingdom that is not of this world.

I suspect church history will eventually record that the American church in the early 21st century was prosperous, building multi-million-dollar facilities and having the resources to provide entertainment and recreational extravaganzas. This is not surprising since the Pied Piper we are following is a national media celebrity living in a 6.5 million dollar mansion on a hill outside Nashville.

We have come a long way from the example of our founder who declared that he had "nowhere to lay his head" (Matthew 9:20) and did not even own a change of clothes.

Why Do You Give Money to Your Church?

It is probably safe to say that money is the most thought about subject for most people. We spend an inordinate amount of time and energy thinking about how to get money, what to do with the money we have, how to survive without money, and myriads of other questions. Money is not only the "root of all evil," but also it is one of the factors that control our lives. If money guides much of our lives as individuals, then it is equally correct to say that money guides much of the life of our churches.

I've never done a survey, but I suspect the most prominent complaint people have about the church centers around the issue of money. You've heard people say, "All that church wants is my money." We frequently hear stories about church leaders abusing money given by members and living extravagant lifestyles.

I have an extensive background in studying and teaching biblical stewardship. Even though my views on the subject changed over the years, the importance of the relationship between the church and money is something I still strive to understand.

The ability of a church to raise funds is strictly dependent upon the intended use of the money. For example, in the matter of capital-fund raising, everyone in the business knows it is easier to raise money for a new sanctuary than for a classroom building. The most challenging capital fund project for raising money is debt elimination. It seems that paying off debt doesn't excite church folks nearly as much as getting a new worship center.

When it comes to raising money for other needs, missions tops the list. Inspiring people to give to share the Gospel, especially in the far corners of the world, is not that difficult. Another good fund-raising project is children. When I was a pastor if we had children who needed money to attend camp all we had to do was make an announcement, and the money would be quickly provided.

Let me ask you to think about an important question: What your church would look like if you took money out of the equation? In other words, if your church had no money, zero income, what would happen?

The changes would be immediate and extensive. Probably the first thing that would happen is that the staff would begin submitting resignation letters. I'm not suggesting that the ministers of your church work for the money only, but for most of them, the church provides their living. They would immediately begin searching for other employment—people do have bills to pay and need to eat.

Perhaps the next significant change for a church with no money is that the utilities would be shut off. It usually takes a month or two of non-payment for this to happen so you could continue meeting for a while. If the church happens to have a mortgage or debt associated with the building then in a few months the bank will begin foreclosure proceedings.

I'm pretty confident that by the time all of this happens, attendance at church functions would be quite small. Only a few diehards would remain, meeting in a cold, dark building with foreclosure notices on the front door.

That's an absurd situation that will never happen, but it does illustrate the dependence of the church on having money. The answer to the question of what happens if you remove money from your church is that it will cease to exist. But that shouldn't be the case. The church was not designed to be reliant upon money for survival. Yet, when you raise the subject of money and the church, many are quick to pick up their Bible and come to the defense of the current situation.

Old Testament Inferences

The most frequently referenced passage concerning giving money to the local church is found in the Old Testament. This is problematic for a straightforward reason—there was no church during Old Testament times. If we are to read scripture from the perspective of context and how it spoke to the historical era that it was written, then I think I'm on safe ground in saying the Old Testament has nothing to tell us about funding the New Testament church.

Of course, the passage most frequently referenced is Malachi 3, specifically verses 7-12:

From the days of your fathers you have turned aside from My statutes and have not kept them. Return to Me, and I will return to you," says the LORD of hosts. 'But you say, 'How shall we return?'"

"Will a man rob God? Yet you are robbing Me! But you say, 'How have we robbed You?' In tithes and offerings. You are cursed with a curse, for you are robbing Me, the whole nation of you! Bring the whole tithe into the storehouse, so that there may be food in My house, and test Me now in this," says the LORD of hosts, "if I will not open for you the windows of heaven and pour out for you a blessing until it overflows. Then I will rebuke the devourer for you, so that it will not destroy the fruits of the ground; nor will your vine in the field cast

its grapes," says the LORD of hosts. "All the nations will call you blessed, for you shall be a delightful land," says the LORD of hosts.

I'm confident when I say there cannot be more than a handful of preachers who have delivered a sermon on this passage more than I have. I mentioned I taught church stewardship for more than a dozen years, and that involved preaching in forty plus churches each year. More often than not, the passage I used during the Sunday morning service was this one from Malachi. When I talk about Malachi 3 and giving by bringing the tithe to the church, I know what I'm talking about.

The idea of bringing a tithe to God is ancient. It can be found in the very first book of the Bible (Genesis 14:20; 28:22). It was practiced by Abraham, four-hundred years before Moses. Bringing a tenth to their god was also a standard exercise in many ancient societies. Man has always used the number ten as a basis for enumerating. The actual number ten represented completeness. Therefore, the tithe symbolized giving our all to God.

The tithe is the most fundamental component of giving to God. There is some speculation that the Old Testament Jews were required to pay three tithes. The first was the "Levite Tithe" (see Numbers 18:21-26), which was given to support the Levites and the maintenance of the Tent of Meeting. The second tithe sometimes called the "Festival Tithe" (see Deuteronomy 14:22-27), was to be brought to Jerusalem and shared in a gigantic festival meal. Finally, there was the tithe which was to be gathered every three years for the aliens, fatherless, and widows (see Deuteronomy 14:28-29), a type of "Welfare Tithe." These three tithes, two full annual tithes and a third tithe every three years, required a total payment of twenty-three and a third percent.

However, there are no compelling reasons to conclude that Israel was expected to pay three tithes. To the contrary, there seems to be sufficient evidence to suggest that the Old Testament Jews paid only one tithe.

The most fundamental reason for rejecting the notion of three separate tithes is no such distinction is made in Scripture. The same terminology is used to describe each of the tithes. The labels such as "Levite Tithe," "Festival Tithe" or "Welfare Tithe" are provided by biblical commentators. Strict adherence to God's Word does not suggest three separate tithes.

Second, the Levites were to be the recipients of each of the tithes (see Numbers 18:21 for "Levite Tithe," Deuteronomy 14:27 for "Festival Tithe" and Deuteronomy 14:29 for "Welfare Tithe"). In other words, the primary purpose of the tithe was to support the Levites "…as their inheritance in return for the work they do while serving at the Tent of Meeting" (Numbers 18:21). In addition to providing for the Levites, the tithe also served the purpose of furnishing food for a national potluck feast and a supplement to the welfare program for the poor.

There would be no reason to bring more than one tithe to support the Levites. According to Numbers 26, the Levites totaled only 3.5% of the nation's population. One tithe would have provided this small tribe with a tenth of the nation's income. A tenth of a nation's gross national product would have been more than sufficient for less than four percent of the population.

Another reason to reject the proposal of three tithes pertains to the "Festival tithe." If the whole nation brought a tenth to the city of Jerusalem, it could not be consumed during a short festival. It would not be feasible, nor very good stewardship, to overindulge by devouring a tithe of the nation's produce at a national feast.

Finally, the New Testament Pharisees provide insight into the first-century understanding of the tithe. Jesus commended the Pharisees for giving one-tenth (see Matthew 23:23; Luke 11:42). The self-righteous Pharisee bragged about giving "a tenth of all I get" (see Luke 18:12). If the law required paying three tithes, naturally the Pharisee would have boasted about twenty-three and a third percent, rather than one-tenth. He seemed content to be identified as a payer of only one tithe.

It may be possible to build a case for one annual tithe and a second tithe given every three years. The tithe described in Deuteronomy 14:28-29 suggests a special tithe to be given every third year to serve as a source of welfare for the poor. However, these words may be unique instructions for the tithe every third year. Rather than the entire tithe going to the Levites, on the third year, it was to be dispersed among the Levites and the poor.

The notion of three separate tithes has been circulated among commentators for a long time. Nevertheless, it is imperative that we remain faithful to Scripture and not the traditions of biblical interpreters. Some have used the idea of three distinct tithes as a means of rendering tithing an obsolete doctrine, not valid for New Testament believers. This is done by identifying the "Levite Tithe" as government taxation, the "Festival Tithe" as an antiquated ritual, and the "Welfare Tithe" as giving to the poor. Since taxes and welfare funding are levied by the government, it is assumed that the tithe is no longer necessary.

The tithe was not a means of taxation. The Old Testament Jews, under the authority of kings, paid taxes in addition to the tithe (see I Samuel 17:25; II Kings 23:35; Ezra 4:13, 20; Nehemiah 5:4). Prior to the monarchy, there was no need for taxation. Israel operated as a theocracy, and there was no government to fund.

Even without a government, Israel did have a welfare system. Provisions for the poor were made by the people, without governmental programs and prodding (see Leviticus 25:25-28, 35-43; Deuteronomy 15:7-11; 24:19-22). The third-year tithe furnished a supplement to these provisions for the needy. God asked His people to bring the tithe in addition to required taxes and supplemental welfare giving.

Malachi specifies the tithe was to be brought to the storehouse. Church leaders often interpret this as a reference to the church. However, as we have already noted, there was no such thing as a church when the prophet Malachi spoke. It was a reference to an actual storehouse, a storage place for meat and produce.

Israel was an agricultural land, and the currency that was tithed was their crops and livestock. It makes sense because the tithe was to provide for the Levites and to feed the poor. It was not the way they collected funds in order to propagate the religion.

It is really unnecessary to study other Old Testament passages to find injunctions about giving money to the church. They are just not found. Old Testament writers had no concept of a church.

The synagogues, which were established during the Babylonian captivity, are perhaps a close relative to today's church. They were local gatherings of Jews for the purpose of studying the Torah, instruction, fellowship, and prayer. However, as they still are today, synagogues were funded by dues collected from members. Tithes and sacrifices always went to the Temple, which has no relation to today's church. If we were to choose the synagogue method of financing for the church, we would charge a membership fee, much like the local Lion's Club or perhaps the YMCA.

There are no Old Testament scriptures that provide guidance about funding the local church.

Church and Money in the New Testament

Since the Old Testament has nothing to say about how to operate the church, we must focus our attention on the New Testament. Since the church today requires money in order to exist, there must be a great deal of guidance on the matter on the pages between Matthew to Revelation. However, there's not.

Sharing of the early church – Acts

Perhaps the passage appealed to most often in support of giving money to the church is the story of the early days of the church recorded in Acts. After the shocking experience at Pentecost where Peter preached, and thousands turned to Jesus, these new believers, the first church, had to do something.

Everyone kept feeling a sense of awe; and many wonders and signs were taking place through the apostles. And all those who had believed were together and had all things in common; and they began selling their property and possessions and were sharing them with all, as anyone might have need. Day by day continuing with one mind in the temple, and breaking bread from house to house, they were taking their meals together with gladness and sincerity of heart, praising God and having favor with all the people. And the Lord was adding to their number day by day those who were being saved. (Acts 2:43-47)

This is not a picture of a massive garage sale and then a pooling of the resources. It describes people sharing what they had with those who had needs. If the need was food, then food was provided, if clothing, then clothing provided. If the need was money, then something was sold in order to provide the money. When people can share financially like this, something extraordinary has happened.

An essential aspect of their fellowship was the way they shared their goods. Property and possessions were disposed in order to provide for those in need. This is not necessarily a common purse but rather a common concern for one another. Those who had were willing to give to those who did not have.

This early church in Jerusalem consisted of many Jews who had traveled a great distance to celebrate the Feast of Pentecost. Upon their conversion to Christ, they remained in the city, without homes or means of support. The need was great for people to share their resources.

A similar experience is recorded two chapters later.

And the congregation of those who believed were of one heart and soul; and not one of them claimed that anything belonging to him was his own, but all things were common property to them. And with great power the apostles were giving testimony to the resurrection of the Lord Jesus, and abundant grace was upon them all. For there was not a needy person among them, for all who were owners of land or houses would sell them and bring the proceeds of the sales and lay them at the apostles' feet, and they would be distributed to each as any had need. (Acts 4:32-35)

The overriding similarity between these two experiences is that the money was given specifically to meet the physical and financial needs of the other believers. They were distributing the resources to help the poor among them.

In no way is this similar to the way churches today collect money. While it is true that today the money is used for believers, but most of it for the purpose of believers having a beautiful building, paid holy men/women, and first-class entertainment. If money is used to feed the hungry or care for the needy, it is a small percentage of what churches receive.

"What a contrast we see between the early church and today's churches. In order to help the poor, the first thing the early church did was sell all their extra land and buildings. The first thing a church does today is buy extra land and buildings."

Offering for Jerusalem – 2 Cor. 8

A second experience of Christian giving in the early church is found in the books of First and Second

Corinthians. To understand these references, we must examine the context. Apparently, the believers in Jerusalem were experiencing difficult times. We know that persecution of Christians began in Jerusalem and spread out from there.

Since they were being persecuted, we can be confident they were not wealthy. The world does not persecute the wealthy. The church in Jerusalem was in crisis—poor and oppressed. If anyone understood persecution in the first century, it would have been Paul. Remember, he is the one who was leading the persecution brigade when he miraculously met Jesus on the Damascus Road.

Paul knew of the suffering of the Jerusalem Christians, so he spread the word to other churches around the world. It seems that when he arrived and reported to the churches in Macedonia, something wonderful happened. The churches of Macedonia included Thessalonica, Berea, and Philippi. These people were not wealthy and in the midst of persecution of their own. But listen to Paul's description that he provided when he wrote to the Corinthians.

Now, brethren, we wish to make known to you the grace of God which has been given in the churches of Macedonia, that in a great ordeal of affliction their abundance of joy and their deep poverty overflowed in the wealth of their liberality. For I testify that according to their ability, and beyond their ability, they gave of their own accord, begging us with much urging for the favor of participation in the support of the saints, and this, not as we had expected, but they first gave themselves to the Lord and to us by the will of God. So we urged Titus that as he had previously made a beginning, so he would also complete in you this gracious work as well. (2 Corinthians 8:1-6)

Paul describes the giving of the Macedonians as "the grace of God." In the midst of their "great ordeal of affliction... and deep poverty" they gave in a way that can only be described as the "wealth of their liberality." He goes on to add that they actually gave beyond their ability, even to the point of begging for the opportunity to give.

They were not giving to put a new roof on the sanctuary or to construct a children's recreation center for themselves. They were giving to ease the suffering of others. Paul was not collecting money so they could meet the annual budget—they had no annual budget. There were (and still are) plenty of reasons for Christians to give that have nothing to do with our own comfort and pleasure.

Earlier, in Paul's first letter to the Corinthians, we are introduced to the collection he is gathering.

Now concerning the collection for the saints, as I directed the churches of Galatia, so do you also. On the first day of every week each one of you is to put aside and save, as he may prosper, so that no collections be made when I come. When I arrive, whomever you may approve, I will send them with letters to carry your gift to Jerusalem; and if it is fitting for me to go also, they will go with me. (1 Corinthians 16:4)

It seems that on a previous visit to Corinth, the believers had committed to Paul they would gather an offering that he could take with him to Jerusalem. Word got back to the Apostle that they were not living up to their commitment to give to others, so he wrote to encourage them to finish what they had started.

These verses have frequently been used to encourage Christians to give money to their church. I know this is true because I did it myself for many years. Yet, I have come to realize this has nothing to do with paying church bills, meeting the church budget, or constructing new church buildings. It is simply what it purports to be—an offering given to relieve the financial suffering of believers in another part of the world.

GIFT TO PAUL

There is one other verse in the New Testament that speaks to the issue of the church and money. We know from the Book of Acts that Paul traveled around the known world preaching the gospel, starting churches, and preaching the Good News of Jesus. However, we also know that he paid his own way, working as a tentmaker.

One of his favorite churches was the one in Philippi. We know this because of the loving way he spoke to them in the Book of Philippians. They were special to him in many ways. They loved him as well, and they demonstrated that love by giving him an offering.

You yourselves also know, Philippians, that at the first preaching of the gospel, after I left Macedonia, no church shared with me in the matter of giving and receiving but you alone; for even in Thessalonica you sent a gift more than once for my needs. (Philippians 4:15-16)

Did you notice that he identified them as the only church that shared with him? In addition, they gave to him "more than once" for his needs, even sending a gift while he was ministering in a neighboring city.

There is not one example of the New Testament church needing money or asking people to give to pay for a building, staff salaries, evangelistic outreach, or any of the things churches typically finance. The few times they were asked to give it was always for the purpose of helping the poor and needy.

The reason for this is quite simple—the early church did not need money.

If your church didn't have money, one of the most noticeable changes would be the loss of a building. Let's examine what that might mean.

Is That Building Really Necessary?

The relationship between the church and buildings has become so intertwined in our thinking that we now define a building as the church. We hear phrases like...

- The church downtown on Fifth Street
- Where do you go to church?
- How many people were in church today?
- I grew up in church
- I want to invite you to come to church with me
- We plan to get married in a church

When we say these things, we know exactly what they mean. They are a reference to a type of building.

The idea of a church being identified with a building is not a biblical concept. The New Testament clearly identifies the church as people who are called out by God and have become followers of Jesus. There is no reference to the church as a building or that there was ever a particular type of building where the church met.

Perhaps the reason the definition of the terms "church" and "building" has become so intertwined is because of how we do church. When a group of Christians gets together, one of the first things they do is talk about how to secure a building. Once they have about twenty-five people gathering, the conversation quickly turns to the necessity of having a building.

Several years ago, a friend and I started a small Bible study group. It quickly became a Sunday evening group gathering for worship, and even though we seldom called ourselves a church, that is essentially what we became. We met in homes, borrowed space from churches, and a myriad of other places.

After a few years, we began talking about having our own place. We were committed to not purchase any property, but we decided we could rent a space that would be all ours. We found a storefront in a great community, secured the financing so it wouldn't require our little group to raise money each month, and signed a six-month lease.

Everything appeared fine until we realized we had created an unanticipated situation. We had a building in a great location that we only used for about two hours per week, on Sunday evening. What were we going to do with the space the rest of the week? It was open and available, but our little group didn't need space every day. For the next six months, I felt the stress of trying to come up with ideas for using our new space. We didn't renew the lease because it was apparent we didn't need a building.

We nearly fell into the trap that snares most churches—the building trap. We think we need a place of our own so we can gather whenever and however we want. But then as soon as we secure that building, we discover that it owns us. It not only takes our money, but it also requires our time and effort. Churches end up spending the majority of what they have on the building.

It would serve us well to understand how this happened.

JESUS AND THE TEMPLE

Some are quick to point out that the Jews had the Temple. It was crucial to their faith. It was a requirement to have a place for their sacrifices and religious duties. They gave sacrificially so Solomon could build the Temple. They fought and gave their lives to protect the building. After it was destroyed, they went back to work and rebuilt it from the ground up. By the time Jesus came along, the Temple in Jerusalem no longer had any connection to Solomon. This one was erected by King Herod in an attempt to appease the Jewish people and keep them on his side.

Jesus was not a fan of the Temple. One of His first acts, according to the Gospel of John, was to drive the money-changers out of the Temple courtyard. Even His own declarations about the Temple got Him in trouble with the Jewish rulers. He claimed that the Temple would be torn down and He would rebuild it in three days. Such a claim drove them crazy. Without a Temple, the Jews as a nation would cease to exist.

The primary purpose of the Temple was to provide a place of sacrifice for the people of God. This structure allowed them to be God's people. However, since Jesus offered the perfect and final sacrifice necessary, the Temple no longer had any reason to exist. The early followers of Jesus, like every follower since, had no need for a building to allow them to meet with God.

However, still today, we hear people describe a portion of the church building as the sanctuary. A sanctuary is a holy place, a place set aside for meeting with God. Typically the sanctuary is where the church gathers for worship on Sunday morning and conducts the worship rituals.

With the crucifixion and resurrection of Jesus, the need for a holy place to be set aside for meeting with God became superfluous. Through the Holy Spirit with us, God is present and available at all times and in places. These are fundamental doctrines of the Christian faith.

Yet, for some reason, we forget about them when it comes to church buildings. The first followers of Jesus were aware they did not need a building for worship or access to God.

THE EARLY CHURCH

It seems the first followers of Jesus were initially drawn to the Temple. On the Day of Pentecost, Peter stood up to preach to the crowds. Obviously, the crowds would have been at or near the Temple; this was a feast day, and people came to Jerusalem to visit the Temple. After the phenomenal response to Peter's sermon, for believers, the Temple was still the natural place to meet and gather. However, that did not last long.

Day by day continuing with one mind in the temple, and breaking bread from house to house, they were taking their meals together with gladness and sincerity of heart... (Acts 2:48)

They quickly moved from the Temple and began to gather in houses where they could share meals.

From this point on, the early followers of Jesus could be found gathering together in homes:

But Saul began ravaging the church, entering house after house, and dragging off men and women, he would put them in prison. (Acts 8:3)

...how I did not shrink from declaring to you anything that was profitable, and teaching you publicly and from house to house... (Acts 20:20)

Greet Prisca and Aquila, my fellow workers in Christ Jesus, who for my life risked their own necks, to whom not only do I give thanks, but also all the churches of the Gentiles; also greet the church that is in their house. (Romans 16:3-5)

The churches of Asia greet you. Aquila and Prisca greet you heartily in the Lord, with the church that is in their house. (1 Corinthians 16:19)

Greet the brethren who are in Laodicea and also Nympha and the church that is in her house. (Colossians 4:15)

Paul, a prisoner of Christ Jesus, and Timothy our brother, To Philemon our beloved brother and fellow worker, and to Apphia our sister, and to Archippus our fellow soldier, and to the church in your house... (Philemon 1:1-2)

If anyone comes to you and does not bring this teaching, do not receive him into your house, and do not give him a greeting... (2 John 1:10)

There is one particular instance that describes them gathering at the Temple, at Solomon's Porch. This was the outer courtyard.

At the hands of the apostles many signs and wonders were taking place among the people; and they were all with one accord in Solomon's portico. (Acts 5:12)

This suggests that occasionally believers would gather in larger public places, but the regular meetings of the church were always in a private home.

The way the early church was structured, homes were the ideal meeting place. Their worship was pure; the only ritual was compatible with an event that took place in every home every day—a meal. "Their central ritual involved a meal that had a domestic origin and setting inherited from Judaism. Indeed, Christians of the first three centuries usually met in private residences that had been converted into suitable gathering spaces for the Christian community… This indicates that the ritual bareness of early Christian worship should not be taken as a sign of primitiveness, but rather as a way of emphasizing the spiritual character of Christian worship."

Even if these early followers of Jesus had the means and opportunity to secure large buildings, there was no need. The purpose of gathering was sharing the supper commemorating Jesus' last supper with His disciples, and encouraging one another in the faith. Both of these activities are done best in small groups, not large auditoriums. Have you ever attended a large congregation where they observed the Lord's Supper? To get it done in a reasonable amount of time requires lots of organization and preparation. However, even then it is nothing like sharing a meal together with fellow believers.

There is some evidence that these houses came in various sizes and layouts. The atrium of a typical Roman villa, or perhaps a dining room in a Greek house, could comfortably accommodate a small Christian community. Remember the story of the young man, Eutychus, who fell asleep while Paul preached. He fell from the third story window of a Greek home.

On the first day of the week, when we were gathered together to break bread, Paul began talking to them, intending to leave the next day, and he prolonged his message until midnight. There were many lamps in the upper room where we were gathered together. And there was a young man named Eutychus sitting on the window sill, sinking into a deep sleep; and as Paul kept on talking, he was overcome by sleep and fell down from the third floor and was picked up dead. But Paul went down and fell upon him, and after embracing him, he said, "Do not be troubled, for his life is in him." When he had gone back up and had broken the bread and eaten, he talked with them a long while until daybreak, and then left. They took away the boy alive, and were greatly comforted. (Acts 20:7-12)

Notice the setting for this event. They gathered to break bread and eat. Paul simply started speaking but prolonged his speaking until midnight. After the boy was raised from the dead, they went back upstairs, shared a meal, and talked until daybreak. They were free to do this because they were meeting in someone's home.

A Change of Plans

When Constantine became Emperor of Rome in 324, he ordered the construction of Christian church buildings. His apparent reasoning was to make the Christian faith a legitimate religion for the Empire. All the other religions had temples and sacred places of worship, which made them quite visible to everyone. On the other hand, Christians were still meeting primarily in homes. Consequently, many people were unfamiliar with the Christian faith.

Although Constantine is credited with putting Christianity on the religious map, he never renounced his allegiance to other religions. It seems he accepted the Christian faith and only added it to his already crowded religious calendar.

Construction of some of the most renowned early church buildings occurred under Constantine's directions. "The most famous Christian 'holy spaces' were St. Peter's on the Vatican Hill (built over the supposed tomb of Peter), St. Paul's Outside the Walls (built over the supposed tomb of Paul), the dazzling and astonishing Church of the Holy Sepulcher in Jerusalem (built over the supposed tomb of Christ), and the Church of the Nativity in Bethlehem (built over the supposed cave of Jesus' birth).

Constantine built nine churches in Rome and many others in Jerusalem, Bethlehem, and Constantinople."

From this point on, the building began to shape church worship and eventually Christian theology. These early church buildings provided for worshippers to sit in rows facing a raised platform. There was a railing that separated the clergy from the laity; remnants are still seen in many churches today. There was also an ornate chair for the Bishop much like the chair found in churches today for the pastor.

It is a fascinating study, one that is worthwhile, to examine how these early structures still influence the way most of us grew up doing church. It also demonstrates the control a building has over a congregation. Not only does it shape our theology, but it also controls the way we spend our money and utilize our time.

Perhaps most distressing is the way it has taken evangelism out of the marketplace and brought it inside the church building. Few Christians share their faith with neighbors and co-workers. Instead, the more brave ones merely invite them to attend church with them. After all, that is where the church does its best evangelism.

The contemporary church understands this very well. They have even developed terminology to help encourage the notion. They speak of having events that are "seeker friendly." Rather than believers seeking out opportunities to share the faith, we are now content with raising enough money to hire professional entertainers who will attract those who are spiritually hungry. We now have a plethora of humongous buildings with massive stages, equal to any professional venue, that serve no other purpose than putting on a show worthy of attracting unbelievers.

The building has become the primary evangelistic resource for a church that is declining in membership and attendance. We are spending inordinate amounts of money on a flawed system. Let me provide an example of how a change in approach to doing church can make an enormous impact on one city.

A New Way Forward

I live in Fort Worth, Texas, a city with a population of 830,000. If the percentages in my town are in accordance with national statistics, then we can assume about 225,000 people attend church at least once or twice a month. It is also estimated that there are 1,300 churches in Fort Worth. Remember, this is a religious part of the country. The largest Christian seminary in the world is located here, so it is not surprising there are so many churches.

This means that the average church attendance is about 150 per week. Several churches have thousands of attendees at multiple sites and events, but there are many more that have a small group barely filling the corner or a large sanctuary.

Let's create a scenario where we get rid of all the church buildings. What are all these believers going to do? If we do what the original followers of Jesus did, they are going to meet in homes. If all these church attendees remained faithful, it would require about 9,000 house churches across the city to accommodate them. This action puts 25 in each group but remember, they don't all attend every week, so that is a workable number.

Equally significant is that it would free up more than $200 million per year that is currently spent on church buildings. In addition, if the current church property is sold, it is probably a good estimate that at least $1 billion would be available for other uses.

Let your imagination run wild about what the church located in Fort Worth could do with that amount of money if we did not need to spend it on a building. Perhaps we could eliminate many of the social problems that plague our community. Countless people could be helped.

Eliminating the church building will create significant changes in the way we do church. However, many of those changes are things that obviously need to happen. For example, the vast majority of ministry efforts of the church take place within the walls of the church building. That makes sense. We have a building so let's use it.

However, those who need the ministry that Christians have to offer are not at the church building. They are in offices, factories, stores, and neighborhoods where we live. If we get rid of church buildings, Christians will be forced out into the world where we belong. We will no longer be able to "invite people to church." Instead, we will take the church to them and meet them where we can best serve their needs.

It seems odd to me that churches work hard to get people to attend large gatherings and then once they are there we encourage them to join a small group. It would be much more effective to involve them in a small group and skip the "big church" step.

The fellowship among believers would be strongly enhanced. It's impossible to go to someone's home and be a part of a small group without getting to know someone. I can't tell you the number of churches I've attended as a visitor, and no one even spoke to me.

Even when someone does offer a "Hi, glad you're here" greeting, it seldom translates into anything of substance. People never ask anything about me other than, "Do you live around here?" It's almost like since I made my way to their church building, they don't need to do anything else.

Imagine how different it would be if you brought someone to your home and introduced them to a small group of gathered believers. We've had people come to our home, and they may come to the conclusion that this type of church is not for them, but they never leave feeling like they didn't get to know anyone or that nobody cared about them being there. It's easy to include people when the gathering is small.

Why Do We Keep Setting Up Our Pastors to Fail?

The role of pastors and church staff has changed considerably during my lifetime. The following is a list of terms we used to describe these folks over the years and how they have evolved.

- Preacher – Pastor – Senior Pastor
- Song Leader – Music Director – Music Minister – Worship Leader – Worship Pastor – Musical Arts Pastor
- Youth Leader – Youth Director – Youth Minister – Youth Pastor – Associate Pastor
- Education Director – Associate Pastor – Executive Pastor

- Children's Worker – Children's Director – Children's Minister – Children's Pastor – Associate Pastor

The change in titles is consistent with the change in power and authority they have been given. We are now at the point where a pastor is considered the Chief Operating Officer (CEO) of the church. Many have seized this new position and prestige and turned themselves into a celebrity.

Perhaps you heard about the young pastor recently who preached a twenty-four-hour sermon. This was not a case of the Holy Spirit falling upon the preacher and inspiring him to keep at it. It was a planned event. He actually designed and advertised the sermon as a means of promoting his new book. By all accounts, he has been a successful pastor, starting and growing a rather large congregation.

He had just finished writing the book and felt like the message would "change lives." Speaking as a writer who has published a few books myself, I agree that if you do not have something important to say that needs to be heard, don't bother writing a book. To be honest, when I found out about this twenty-four-hour sermon, my first thought was that I am glad I have lived long enough that people have forgotten all the dumb stuff I did in my twenty's. Hopefully, this young man will live long enough as well.

The underlying issue of this whole business is preachers performing some kind of stunt in order to attract attention and draw a crowd. It raises the question of celebrity preachers. The basic definition of celebrity is quite simple. A celebrity is someone who is widely known. We have elevated the idea of being a celebrity to new heights. There are magazines, websites, and television programs that exist for the sole purpose of revealing insights about celebrities.

It's a vicious cycle–do something that is widely noticed, appear in a magazine or newspaper, other magazines take note, people follow you around, do something else, everyone notices, get on more magazine covers, do something stupid, one last burst of notoriety, loose all your friends. The amazing thing is that so many folks are striving to be celebrities it is almost like a chosen profession for some–What do you want to be when you grow up? A celebrity!

I do not have a problem with celebrity preachers. The issue that concerns me is preachers who strive to be celebrities without realizing the cost. I think it is safe to say that Billy Graham was a celebrity preacher. He was very well-known all around the world. However, he became famous by preaching. His celebrity was a by-product of his work. I didn't know him personally, but I never felt like he sought out the celebrity status, although he certainly knew how to utilize it. There have been many celebrity preachers throughout history–Charles Spurgeon, George

Whitefield. It might even be correct to say that Jesus was a celebrity preacher in his day.

Since we live in such a media-saturated society, there are numerous celebrity preachers today. I saw a recent article that listed twenty-two in the city of Houston. I don't know if I would consider them all celebrities because I don't think most of us have heard of them, but they are well-known in certain large circles.

When a person becomes a celebrity, it changes everything about their life. They are constantly faced with the temptation of ego. I don't know, but I suspect it is hard to remain humble when you regularly see your face on magazine covers, or read stories about yourself in the newspaper, or see your name on top of a list of speakers at large conferences. It also exposes everything you say or do to questioning. You must be ready to explain why you spent money in a certain way, why you made a particular statement, what you believe about a subject, or give your opinion on something you know nothing about.

Celebrity preachers are also susceptible to having their sins exposed. We are all aware they sin, they are celebrities, not deities, and when everyone is watching so closely, their sins will be made known. The truth is that we don't expect them to be perfect, but we hope they will not sexually molest others, seek extravagant lifestyles, or try to cover up secret activities. It's tough to be a celebrity preacher and remain faithful.

I read a story about a preacher once who was a very persuasive and powerful man. In fact, he possessed such a gift from God that he actually healed a man who had been crippled from birth. The man stood up and walked, and everyone heard about it and believed it was true. Consequently, the crowds believed the preacher and his associate were gods and brought great offerings to them. In spite of the preacher's protests, his reputation spread and ultimately angered the religious establishment. These religious leaders grabbed the preacher, drug him out of town, beat him, and left him for dead. End of story you might think.

However, the preacher rose up (perhaps he was not completely dead, I don't know), and returned to the city. At this point, he could have been on the front of every newspaper and magazine cover in the region. He could have used his celebrity status to proclaim Jesus to the masses. He would have been known as the miracle-working preacher who came back from the dead. No need for a publicist. Talk about having something to say!

Instead of seeking celebrity status, this preacher and his associate left town the next day in order to carry the Gospel to another place. He wanted nothing to do with the worshipping crowds. In case you are a little rusty on your New Testament, this is a story about Paul taken from the fourteenth chapter of Acts. Paul seemed to understand the danger of being placed on a pedestal and wanted nothing to do with it. The problem with pedestals is that they are normally quite wobbly.

Before we castigate preachers for striving after celebrity status, we need to realize that they are merely doing what the church expects from them. The church requires a pastor who is able to attract crowds while providing direction and guidance for the entire church operation. Sunday morning events are intended to be the main visible function of the church; the time when the church has the greatest opportunity to impact the community. In order for this to happen, the pastor must be an excellent communicator and/or showman.

In fact, the pastor has become such a crucial part of the church that if the position were to be eliminated, the church would cease to function. Churches are aware of this potentiality. When a pastor does resign for some reason, the church will recruit an "interim pastor" to help them survive until they can secure a more permanent person to fill the position.

In an article titled, "Expressing Christ in an Organic Church," Mark Lake writes these words: "Paul says in Ephesians 3:8 that there are "unsearchable riches" in Christ. Imagine with me that the Louvre Museum in Paris is a picture of all of the riches that are in Christ. The Louvre has approximately 35,000 exhibits in its massive museum grounds, not to mention the architecture alone is stunning. Many of the most famous pieces of artwork in history are housed within these walls.

"Now, imagine a group of people setting out to explore and experience the riches of this museum. To give 5 minutes to each of the 35,000 pieces of art would take 243 twelve hour days! Picture this group entering the museum in awe of its beautiful architecture. They gather around a famous art display and take in its beauty and uniqueness. After some time, they share with each other what aspects of this piece of art stood out to them and how it affected them. As they go around the group taking turns sharing, they find that no one saw quite the same thing, even though they were all certainly looking at the same piece. Some were astounded by the colors. Others were captivated by the fine detail in the work. Some were focused on one particular aspect, such as the expression on a face. Some wondered about the meaning of the painting. Others pondered the artist's motivation for the piece. As the group shared their varied insights, everyone saw much more of the artwork than any one person saw themselves. As the group moves through the museum, gazing upon the beautiful art and sharing with each other, they grow closer as they share together and even begin to see the artwork from other people's perspective.

"...Imagine if the same group went to the Louvre Museum, but when they made it into the foyer, they elected only one person to go in and view the artwork and then come back and share with the group what he alone saw. Without entering the museum together, the group's ability to fully understand what the one person saw is difficult and limited. Week after week, they gather in the foyer and listen to this one person describe more of what he has seen. As the weeks and years pass, this person appears to be so much of an expert in the Louvre artwork; the group is intimidated to think about going inside themselves, lest they be expected to come back and expound on what they saw as well as the expert does."

The church has arrived at the point where the pastor is expected to bring a word directly from God every time he/she enters the pulpit or sits on a stool. In addition, the pastor is also expected to provide spiritual direction for the congregation, oversee the physical requirements of the church's facilities, and make sure everyone is baptized, married, and buried. The congregation is made to feel like they are doing their part if they provide the financing. If you really want to be involved, you can volunteer to help out occasionally.

Dare I say the church has turned the pastor into a type of priest, one who is our direct representative to God and God's direct spokesperson to us? The pastor does what we can't do because he/she has been "called" and "ordained."

There has been a great deal of discussion throughout the history of the church about the existence and role of pastors, elders, deacons, and bishops. Regardless of the conclusion you choose, there is not any suggestion that one person is to act in the role of what we expect from our pastors today. It seems that each church is to have some combination of prophets, evangelists, pastors, and teachers "for the equipping of the saints for the work of service, to the building up of the body of Christ" (Ephesians 4:12).

By bestowing so much authority on our pastors, we are setting them up to fail. It is impossible to live up to all the expectations, so they are tempted to cut corners, cheat, or manipulate, or if they are really honest, resign.

However, if a person were asked to shepherd (what the word "pastor" actually means) a group of 25-30 people, then he/she could do it effectively. Also, as we have already discovered, the task of constructing and maintaining a building is eliminated from the portfolio, and there is no need to play favorites in order to guarantee a salary. What we would have is a pastor with the time, energy, and resources to be a good shepherd.

This pastor would be in a position to equip others in building up the body. Imagine what it would be like to have a pastor to encourage and train you in how to do ministry, or have the opportunity to share with others in the church from your own personal experience with God. How much more would you learn if you could hear the experiences and wisdom of the entire group, instead of the edicts of one pastor?

The church needs, and will always need spiritual guidance. Without a shepherd, the sheep will be scattered and defenseless. But think about the analogy. A shepherd leads the herd to a pasture where there is food and water.

He doesn't take it upon himself to feed every lamb. They are left to themselves to find nourishment. If they struggle, get injured, or find themselves in trouble, the shepherd will come to their rescue.

The church has pushed the analogy too far. We want the pastor, especially if we bestow the title of "Senior Pastor," to be responsible for everything. The result is quite apparent today. Those pastors who were particularly good at the task are building mega churches. Those who are not so good, but still capable, are serving in mid-sized churches. However, those who are not as gifted and talented, find themselves in small churches, holding on for survival, or at least until retirement. Obviously, this is a generalization, but it is not far from the truth.

Imagine if a pastor was only responsible for the care and nourishment of 20 to 30 people. The fellowship of the group would be dynamic, the learning curve would be steep, and the reputation of the church would be glowing—much like the early church in the first century. Those churches were not perfect, but they eventually changed the world.

If you attend a church of more than two or three hundred attendees, it's likely the pastor doesn't even know your name or even that you have never met the pastor in person. Aware of this possibility, the church hires associate pastors who are responsible for various groups of people in the hope of ministering to everyone. Even then, people fall through the cracks, and no one knows when they're hurting or when they need ministry.

Hospital visitation is not done out of concern for the individual but because that particular pastor's name was on the hospital visitation board for the day in the church office. Family financial needs are not addressed because no one at the church knows the family well enough to realize they are struggling.

Speaking from personal experience after visiting dozens of churches in our neighborhood, visitors will seldom get a personal contact. I can only recall one time that a person from the church knocked on our front door or called to introduce themselves or welcome us to their church.

The reason this is significant is because the opportunity to build a relationship is left up to the outsider. As the visitor, it is apparently my responsibility to make an effort to attend a special information class, or request a newsletter, or stop by the church office, or sign up for a small group. It has become a numbers game. There are so many people that they don't have the time or the manpower to focus on a single individual or family. To be honest, I feel just as welcome at the Wal-Mart when the greeter meets me at the door. At least at Wal-Mart, they will occasionally ask if I need help when I'm looking lost in the wrong aisle.

The institutional church has become so much about numbers that it's impossible to be about people. Pastors are not expected to shepherd individual sheep. They are more like ranch foremen who oversee a large ranch with sheep all over the place.

To ask a pastor to oversee a multi-million-dollar organization, supervise a multi-person staff, tend to the spiritual needs of a large congregation, and be responsible for a dynamic presentation every week is far beyond any description given in scripture. Few pastors today function as shepherds. Instead, they are more of a business leader.

The Apostle Peter offers these words of guidance for the pastor: "Be shepherds of God's flock that is under your care, watching over them--not because you must, but because you are willing, as God wants you to be; not pursuing dishonest gain, but eager to serve..." (1 Peter 5:2). This task is virtually impossible if the flock contains more than a hundred souls.

When Churches Go Wrong

As I mentioned earlier, I was raised in the home of a pastor, I worked as a pastor myself for 13 years, and I was a consultant to pastors for another 20 years. I understand something of what it means to be a pastor. I have also observed many pastors who have failed. In doing so, they have not only embarrassed themselves, but also often ruined their family, and clearly damaged the reputation of the church.

The expectations we have placed on our pastors is the primary reason for this abundance of failures. We understand they are human, but at the same time, we expect that they will be able to walk on water. Jamin Goggin said, "We have accepted that leaders can minister in their strength and narcissism and still bear good fruit, and we have rejected the one who said, "My grace is sufficient for you, for my power is made perfect in weakness" (2 Cor. 12:9). These leaders try to sow in the flesh to reap in the Spirit, and we celebrate them for doing so. That is either folly or delusion. What we sow we will reap; it is one of the most repeated and fundamental axioms in Scripture (Gal. 6:7-8).

About twenty years ago, one of the funniest things I have ever heard about happened to my father. To understand this event you have to know that my father had an artificial leg, having lost his right leg during the Big War in the Pacific. This loss occurred before I was born, so I didn't know him when he had both legs. Having what we always called a "wooden leg" was no big deal for any of us, although they quit making them out of wood a long time ago.

Daddy always liked to have fun with his circumstances, and he would often pretend to be knocking on some little kid's head while simultaneously rapping on his leg, making it sound like they had a wooden head. At night he would stand his leg in the corner of the bathroom, which occasionally freaked some folks out when we had friends spend the night. Daddy knew how to make the best out of a tough situation.

The incident I remember so vividly occurred in the foyer at City Hall in Amarillo, Texas. He and my mother had just moved into town, and he went to get the utilities turned on at their new house. It was a rainy day, an unusual thing in the Texas panhandle. Any kind of precipitation always made walking with a wooden leg a little treacherous. If you have ever tried to walk without steady support, you know that two of the worst enemies are ice and wet tile.

As he stepped into the building foyer, his right leg, the artificial one, slipped out from under him and down he went. I'm sure it was an event worthy of a YouTube moment. Daddy was uninjured, but he had a serious problem. As a result of the fall, his wooden leg came loose from his stump. Now he had a conundrum. His leg was dangling in his pants, and he couldn't put it back on nor could he slide it out of his pants. Remember, the upper part of your leg will probably not fit through your pant leg.

His leg was held on by creating suction to his stump. This was accomplished by using a stocking. Daddy had a stocking in the glove compartment of his car, so he had one of several helpful observers retrieve it for him. However, in order to put his leg back on, he had to drop his pants. If you have ever been in a difficult situation, you have discovered that people want to help. Such was the case. A group of men gathered around him, blocking him from view, while he slid his pants to the floor, reattached his leg, and then put his pants back on. By the time he was finished, a sizable crowd had gathered in the City Hall foyer.

A valuable lesson can be gleaned from my father's experience–the easiest way to draw a crowd is to drop your pants in public.

We have seen this truth demonstrated time and again, from Lady Godiva to Madonna, to Kim Kardashian. I don't mean to imply that seeing my father in his briefs is equivalent to viewing an attractive pop icon, but they both demonstrate how to gather a crowd. In my father's case it was in the foyer of city hall, but for others, it is on Internet websites and checkout line magazines.

All of this is based on a fundamental tenet of human nature. We are attracted to sensational, unusual, bizarre, and tragic events. Everyone likes a good show. Accidents always draw a crowd, not because everyone wants to help, but because everyone wants to see. Do something out of this world and folks will come. Today, it's even more effective if you sprinkle it with some sex.

I have witnessed some unusual attempts by churches to attract crowds of people. Most of them pale in comparison to what happened a few years ago just down the road. The pastor of a Megachurch and his wife climbed up to the roof of their church building and spent twenty-four hours together in bed. I don't know why there is a bed on the church roof, but apparently, it is there.

In a stunt reminiscent of flagpole sitting from early in the 20th century, this pastor and his wife spent twenty-four hours in the bed. Alvin "Shipwreck" Kelly originated flagpole sitting, and his initial foray lasted thirteen

Why I Quit Going to Church

hours and thirteen minutes, far short of the twenty-four hours of church bed sitting. Unlike Kelly in 1924, this experience was broadcast live on the Internet.

All of this is carefully orchestrated to coincide with the release of the pastor's book. It seems this is nothing more than a marketing stunt to drive customers to Amazon where they can purchase the book for $21.95. As usual, it's all about the money. Don't we have a term for those who use sex for money?

This pastor is more than fifty years old so he might need to get a prescription for Viagra before making that climb to the church roof. Hey, we might get the pharmaceutical company to sponsor the event and generate an even bigger payday. After all, God wants us to have good sex. In his own words, sex is about "recreation and enjoyment." It seems only natural that God would approve of popping a couple of little blue pills to heighten the enjoyment. I hope they had a doctor on call in case he has one of those four-hour problems.

I've heard more than one Youth Minister tell me that their greatest fear was finding a couple of high school kids in their youth group having sex in the church basement. Now it seems they should even be more concerned about the kids finding the pastor and his wife having sex on the church roof. It's not all bad news though; at least the pastor is not gay.

Call me old-fashioned, but I have a difficult time understanding why we need to have a bed at church. I've seen pictures of this pastor's house, and it appears there are plenty of bedrooms to be had. What's he going to tell his kids when he and his wife walk out the front door on Friday night, "We'll see you in twenty-four hours, your Mom and I are going up to the church for some fun" as he gives a subtle wink. Talk about being scarred for life—I hope they had a counselor standing by.

Another thing—how does he get his wife to go along with this stuff? It's quite common for guys to brag about their sexual exploits, but usually, women are a little more discreet, especially a pastor's wife. To listen to your pastor's wife talk about her bedroom exploits is only slightly more comfortable than listening to your mother have the same conversation.

I guess the biggest question I have is what does this have to do with lifting up Jesus? Unless there are some considerable gaps in the New Testament record, Jesus never had sex. The Apostle Paul suggested that if you are not currently married, you should stay single to avoid the complications of marital life. I am not suggesting that sex is a bad thing nor do I mean to imply the Bible has nothing to offer on the subject. But please, can we be a little more discreet?

However, this is the way many of the fastest growing churches do it. They are held up as the model for how to reach people with the Gospel. It is the way some do church growth. It is no longer good enough to gather on Christmas Eve, light a few candles and worship the birth of our Savior. No, we need live camels and donkeys, laser light shows, extravagant gift giveaways, and Hollywood-type productions. Sure, you can congregate a handful of people to study the spiritual warfare passage in Ephesians, but what if you drive an army tank on stage for the Sunday morning show. Many in the church have figured out the best way to attract a crowd is to do something like dropping your pants.

There appears to be a great deal of "pants-dropping" happening at church today. Several churches are getting in on the practice of sponsoring cage fights. I guess the rationale is to beat the hell out of people so they can find Jesus. Another pastor popped up out of a casket to deliver his Easter sermon. Churches have also given away cars, television sets, and countless other goodies to attract people to special events.

As early as 1977, Martin Marty, a liberal religious scholar, referred to the trend as "Fundies in their Undies." Although this is not a new trend, today's speed of communication and access to information has made it much more wide-spread.

When a church has financial obligations to meet they must turn up the pressure on staff to generate more and more income. This means the pastor is less of a shepherd to the flock and more of a CEO of a small company. The value of the pastor is not going to be determined by ministry or spiritual leadership, but by the number of butts in the sanctuary seats and dollars in the offering plates. It places an almost irresistible pressure on the pastor to set aside the work of the Gospel for the task of fundraising.

At the age of 21, I sensed a call from God. A call from God is difficult to explain. I believe that every follower of Christ is called to evangelize, encourage, and explain the faith. But, some of us are the recipients of an assignment to give the majority of our lives to the work of the Gospel. In the numerous years since that call, I have been a pastor for only about fourteen of those years. However, at any point in my life, if you ask me what I do, the answer has always been, "I'm a preacher!"

Preaching has not always paid the bills. I have made a living by being a salesman, consultant, denominational employee, writer, and book publisher. There have been times when I preached in three to five churches a week. There have been other times when I went three to five months between preaching opportunities. But it does not matter how often I preach, at any point in my life, if you ask me what I do, the answer has always been, "I'm a preacher!"

As I neared graduation from college, the head of the Religion department told me it would be challenging for me to have an opportunity to pastor a church because of the wheelchair. At seminary, they excused me from preaching requirements and tried to steer me toward counseling, assuming that I was not physically able to preach. After thirteen successful years as a pastor, when it was time to move on, churches were not interested in even talking to me, in spite of glowing recommendations from denominational leaders. However, it does not matter who thinks I can be a preacher, at any point of my life, if you ask me what I do, the answer has always been, "I'm a preacher!"

In spite of being frequently encouraged to pursue another career, it is the call of God that has shaped my life and determined my experiences. I have given my life to pursuing this call of God. I am enamored and overwhelmed with this call of God. I can honestly declare to you today that I have exhausted my resources striving to be faithful to this call of God.

Because of that, not only am I deeply in love with following Jesus, but I am also deeply in love with the church – the Body of Christ – the physical presence of my Lord and Savior. Not only have I spent years studying Christ, but I have also spent years studying the church. I have preached in nearly five hundred pulpits, provided extensive consultation with more than two hundred pastors, and read books and articles about the church vociferously. Needless to say, I have a lot of opinions about the church and church leaders.

To be honest, I am not very optimistic about the American church, which is exceptional for me since I tend to be the ultimate optimist. I not only see the glass as half full, I normally see it as flowing over the top. But, I am concerned about the church today, and one of my primary concerns is that we have taken the call of God and turned it into a career.

The tenth chapter of Matthew is a record of Jesus' "call" to the Twelve. He called them and then sent them out with a task. Essentially, He gave them three tasks – to preach, heal, and trust. It is the work of the church, and He has been calling men and women to the task ever since.

These twelve Jesus sent out after instructing them: "Do not go in the way of the Gentiles, and do not enter any city of the Samaritans; but rather go to the lost sheep of the house of Israel. "And as you go, preach, saying, 'The kingdom of heaven is at hand.' "Heal the sick, raise the dead, cleanse the lepers, cast out demons. Freely you received, freely give. "Do not acquire gold, or silver, or copper for your money belts, or a bag for your journey, or even two coats, or sandals, or a staff; for the worker is worthy of his support. Matthew 10:5-10

However, there is a prevalent trend in the church today to turn the call of God into a career. The dictionary definition of "career" is an occupation undertaken for a significant period of a person's life and with opportunities for progress. Basically, it is the answer to the question, "What do you want to be when you grow up?" The answer–I want to be a doctor, lawyer, baseball player, or preacher! It is a chosen profession for the purpose of providing an acceptable living. This is what happens when you turn a calling from God into a career.

CHANGE THE MESSAGE

When Jesus called the Twelve, He sent them out with a specific message–they were to preach that "the kingdom of heaven is at hand." Theologians have written numerous volumes on the meaning of the kingdom of heaven, and seminary students actually read some of them.

Since I must operate in the real world (not the world of academia) let me offer my real-world understanding of this task. Obviously, "kingdom" speaks of the place where the King rules. Since it is the "kingdom of heaven" then it must be a reference to the place where God in heaven rules. The message that those who have been called are to proclaim is that the King of heaven is here.

Put yourself in first century Palestine, a land controlled by Caesar. Caesar is the king. If you are tending your field or shopping in the local market and you hear the announcement that "Caesar is here!" What would you do? It would make an immediate difference in your life. It would be a call to change what you are doing and possibly even change who you are. Something significant is about to happen!

The message of the church is that God, the creator and sustainer of the universe, has broken into history, sent His Son to open up a relationship with us, and is ready to radically alter our lives. It is a message of redemption and transformation. Like a first century Jew hearing that Caesar is coming down the road, it is a message that is shocking and will impact every area of our lives.

However, the announcement that the kingdom of heaven is here is no longer the primary message of the church. Instead, it has been replaced with, "Let me tell you how to be successful." I did a Google search on the phrase, "How to be a successful Christian" and received nearly 41 million results. A search of the phrase "kingdom of heaven" did reveal 17 million results, but the first two pages concerned an R-rated movie about the 12th century Crusades.

The message has been changed to make it less offensive and more acceptable to our 21st-century world. The rationale is that in order to get large numbers of people into our church buildings, we must tell them what they want to hear. We call it "seeker-sensitive," but in reality, it has become "seeker-driven."

- People want to know how to have a good family life so let's offer a series of sermons explaining what to do to make it happen.
- People are struggling with their finances so let's provide a workshop on managing your money.
- People are fighting depression so let's tell them how to overcome despair.

There is nothing wrong with any of these (and God knows I have done my share), but this is far less than the call we were given. We have been called to proclaim a much more important message than how to get along better in this world. Our message is an announcement to rearrange our lives according to a different world–there is a new king!

Jesus has asked us to invite folks to participate in a new world, but too often we try to help them be more comfortable in the existing world. The problem with the church today is that we have changed the message so that it sounds as if Christianity is nothing more than living the good life.

Change the Method

The method that Jesus gave to those He called is startling. They were to "heal the sick, raise the dead, cleanse the lepers, cast out demons," I'll be honest, this sounds more like a Benny Hinn crusade than anything I'm comfortable with.

Apparently, the disciples were not as sophisticated as me. They went out preaching the kingdom and doing the works. Even before the Pentecostal gift of the Holy Spirit, the disciples proclaimed the message; using the methods they were given. Later we are told that they came back to report what they had seen.

I am going to say very bluntly that we do not see much sick-healing, dead-raising, unclean-cleansing, or demonic-outcasting today. What has happened? I think we have changed the method, primarily as a result of changing the message.

Once the message became more about being comfortable or successful rather than living in a different kingdom, it was easy to change the methods. If the message is nothing more than feel good and enjoy the best this world has to offer, we do not need to worry ourselves with healing, raising, and cleansing.

The method becomes more about comfort, entertainment, and education.

Since the message is to live the good life, it's necessary to provide comfort in a very uncomfortable world. We have turned our churches into sanctuaries where folks can go to have all their needs met without rubbing elbows with unpleasant people and challenging situations. The really "dynamic" churches provide all the sports leagues and entertainment venues for our children, relationship needs for the entire family, and all the God-stuff we need in our lives – all within the confines of a colorfully designed state of the art facility that makes us want to relax and stay a while.

While running the risk of being accused of taking the wrong side of the worship war, let me simply say that much of what happens when the church gathers today is more about entertainment than anything else. That is why we need monolithic congregations because providing the necessary entertainment is expensive.

A third aspect of our method is to educate. Listen to this quick list of real sermon topics:

- Living in the Sweet Spot of Success
- Taking Steps Toward Making Change
- Opening and Closing the Right Doors
- Avoiding Personal Burnout
- Twelve Keys to Abundant Living
- Save Me I'm Drowning in Debt

These sermons are very typical of what happens in church today, and it seems clear that our approach is to help people enjoy the here and now rather than arranging for life in a new kingdom.

The Hospice Movement began in this country in the 1960's. If you have ever had a loved one experience the process of dying under the watchful eye of a hospice professional, you know it is a valuable resource. Caring, well-trained people are there to help the entire family be comfortable and at ease with the entire process of dying and death. In my opinion, hospice care is a very good thing.

However, when it comes to the work of the church, providing hospice care is not a good thing. Yet, that is what I think we are doing. We are providing comfort for those who are dying in the wrong kingdom.

CHANGE THE MOTIVE

The final thing I want to mention about changing a call into a career is that it happens when we change our motive. This is really the heart of the message by Jesus in this passage, and it is the central focus.

Several years ago I was working with a young pastor, and the subject of pastors from different generations came up. I was not quite old enough to be his father, but not far from it. He was curious about the approaches by pastors in different generations. I provided an example by asking a question–when you spoke to this church about being their pastor, did you ask about taking time off–vacation days, and days off, etc.?

Almost incredulously he said, "Of course, what's wrong with that!"

I quickly assured him there was probably nothing wrong with asking, but there was a huge difference. I would have never asked. In fact, at his age, if a church was interested in me being their pastor, I would have never asked if they were even going to pay me.

There is nothing wrong with paying the preacher, in fact, Jesus makes it very clear in our text that the workman is worthy of payment. God provides, and for pastors, He normally provides through a salary given by the church. But we have to be careful with motive.

When I was the pastor of a very small Texas Baptist church, every spring we would receive a survey from the state office. The survey sought for answers about pastor's salary and other benefits. The information was compiled by the Stewardship Department and then provided for help in putting together the church budget. I dutifully filled out my survey every year.

Later, when I went to work in the Stewardship Department, I learned that the survey was discontinued. I was told by the man in charge at the time that the survey created a problem. Pastors who were receiving a salary that was higher than the average were upset. It seems that when their church leaders compared what they were paying their pastor compared to other churches, they wanted to make some changes.

When Jesus issued the call, He clearly said, "Do not acquire..." But, the evidence that we have turned this calling into a career is that it has been changed to, "What's in it for me?"

I'm going to be honest-choosing the ministry is not a bad career move. The pay is much better than it used to be, time off is good, most churches provide decent benefits, including insurance and retirement.

In times past, joining the army was seldom seen as an excellent career choice for most people. However, times have changed. My youngest son, with a Master's Degree in Forensic Psychology, joined the army. He didn't make the decision because he wanted to be Rambo, it is merely a good career move for what he wants to do.

The same is true for the modern church in America-it can be a good career move.

In Fort Worth where I live, there have been two very well known pastors caught up in scandals this past year over the ownership of a private jet. Some have turned the call of God into a very lucrative career. However, that is not my primary concern.

I am concerned about pastors of small and medium size churches who have locked themselves into a lifestyle that requires significant financial resources to maintain. They have put themselves in a position where they can no longer follow the call but must first seek a career. Their biggest concern has become doing whatever is necessary to ensure that the offerings at church stay at a certain level. Decisions are made, not necessarily on what is best for the church but for what is most profitable.

I am also concerned about soon to be seminary graduates who will be tempted to allow the lure of "gold, or silver, or copper for your money belts, or a bag for your journey, or even two coats, or sandals, or a staff" distract them from the place where God has called them.

If you are a pastor and have been called, it is imperative that you keep yourself in a position that allows you to respond to that call. That means you must keep yourself free from relationships and obligations that will keep you from going and doing.

There are some very practical considerations resulting from these words of Jesus. First, if you plan to be in ministry, plan accordingly –

- Avoid excessive debt – It is common for a seminary student to graduate with a substantial burden of student loans and other debt. The problem is that it becomes challenging to find a church that can afford to pay enough to allow these debts to be serviced.
- Adopt a lifestyle that can be supported by a church, without being burdensome to the church – do not expect the church to make it possible for you to live according to your desires, be willing to accept what they can do or be willing to seek other sources of income.
- Accept the possibility that you will have less of the world's stuff than most – I think it is safe to say that if you respond to the call of God for ministry, you might have to turn you back on the great American Dream. In most cases they are incompatible.
- Make sure your spouse makes the same commitments – you can't do this without the support of the most important person in your life.
- Consider earning your living doing something other than ministry – This has been the normal practice throughout most of the history of the church and is still the practice in most of the world.

Recently, I read an excellent book by Eugene Peterson, "The Pastor: A Memoir." He provides a valuable observation about what has taken place in the church.

...one of the most soul-damaging phrases that has crept into the Christian vocabulary is "full-time Christian work." Every time it is used, it drives a wedge of misunderstanding between the way we pray and the way we work, between the way we worship and the way we make a living.

One of the achievements of the Protestant Reformation was a leveling of the ground between clergy and laity. Pastors and butchers had equal status before the cross. Homemakers were on a par with evangelists. But insidiously that level ground eroded as religious professionals claimed the high ground, asserted exclusive rights to "full-time Christian work," and relegated the laity to part-time work on weekends under pastoral or priestly direction. A huge irony—the pastors were hogging the show, and the laity were demeaned with the adjectives "mere," "only," or "just": "He or she is just a layperson."

Most of what Jesus said and did took place in a secular workplace in a farmer's field, in a fishing boat, at a wedding feast, in a cemetery, at a public well asking a woman he didn't know for a drink of water, on a country hillside that he turned into a huge picnic, in a court room, having supper in homes with acquaintances or friends. In our Gospels, Jesus occasionally shows up in synagogue or temple, but for the most part he spends his time in the workplace. Twenty-seven times in John's Gospel Jesus is identified as a worker: "My Father is *still working, and I also am working" (Jn. 5:17). Work doesn't take us away from God; it continues the work of God. God comes into view on the first page of our scriptures as a worker. Once we identify God in his workplace working, it isn't long before we find ourselves in our workplaces working in the name of God.*

If you have been called, then you have been called to the work—the work of proclaiming the coming of God's kingdom by healing, raising, and cleansing. It is essentially the work of the church. However, if you put yourself in a position of needing the ministry to provide you with a particular lifestyle, it is likely that you will adapt the work of the church to serve your purpose. Here is the way that progression works typically:

- Need more money
- Attract larger crowds, they bring more money
- Provide services that draw larger crowds
- Need more money to pay for these services

It has taken me until my 60's to understand this situation. I now understand that I am not dependent upon the church meeting my financial needs—that is God's work. Until you know this truth, you will not be free to follow the call that God has issued to you. "Do not acquire gold, or silver, or copper for your money belts, or a bag for your journey, or even two coats, or sandals, or a staff; for the worker is worthy of his support.

When the Church Chooses Country over Christ

If the American church today had official colors, they would be red, white, and blue along with a sprinkling of stars. It is almost surprising that we don't actually name it "The American Church," rather than Baptist Church, or Methodist Church, or Presbyterian Church. It seems the church is more proud of its American heritage than with its denominational or historical heritage.

Several years ago I was scheduled to fill the pulpit for a pastor who was planning to be out of town on vacation. When I accepted the invitation, I simply checked my calendar to make sure I was available without noticing that it was Memorial Day Weekend. To be honest, as long as our family had no plans of being out of town on Sunday, it didn't matter if it was a national holiday.

I prepared a sermon and showed up early, ready to preach.

Until the morning service began, I hadn't given a thought to the fact it was Memorial Day. But the entire morning event was planned as an American celebration; patriotic songs, readings, and prayers. It was evident that I was the only one there that morning not prepared to pledge my allegiance to America.

I'm not denying that being an American citizen is a great thing. Like nearly every other American, there is no other place I'd rather live. However, that is not the reason the church gathers. America is not to be our object of worship on Sunday mornings (or any other morning for that matter).

To be honest, I'm often embarrassed by American Christians, and it is not because of sinful behavior, but by inconsistent beliefs. For example, there are many...

- Christians who are more interested in permission to carry a gun than laying down their life for another.
- Christians who are willing to support a politician whose lifestyle, words, and actions are incompatible with what Christ called us to be.
- Christians who are willing to kill to protect their Second Amendment rights, but have no idea what the Second Commandment says.

- Christians who insist on being tolerant, but then quickly scoff at conservatives and fundamentalists.
- Christians who think they know all the answers because they have read the Bible.
- Christians who believe the life of faith is all about believing and nothing about doing.
- Christians who are hateful while claiming to hate the sin but love the sinner.

Many people in the history of this country have given up their life in the fight for freedom of speech. It is a freedom that should never be taken lightly because it is not available in many parts of the world. In fact, I feel safe in saying it is the most essential freedom for a free society. If I were a dictator of a country, it would be the first freedom I would remove. It is even more crucial than the right to bear arms. Many countries without gun control do not have freedom, but there are very few places where they have freedom of speech but still live under oppression.

We all learned the phrase, "The pen is mightier than the sword" in elementary school. It has proven true over and over again. Take for example the recent upheavals that have been exacerbated as the result of social media and the ability to communicate. The pen, or Twitter, or Facebook has proven to be far more powerful than weapons. As long as we have the freedom of speech, we will be free.

Yet, freedom of speech is not absolute. You cannot scream "fire" in a crowded theater. You cannot lie under oath. To speak an untruth that harms the reputation of another is also not allowed. We have learned that freedom of speech, like any freedom, can be used to excess. It is a treasured possession that is worth protecting.

However, Christians do not have freedom of speech, not even in America. In saying this, I am not referring to some "left-wing conspiracy" to rob us of our basic rights as citizens. If you have cast your lot with Jesus, then your citizenship is in a different kingdom–you are a citizen of the kingdom of God. It's like the old song said, "This world is not my home, I'm just passing through…"

Citizens of God's kingdom do not have freedom of speech. In other words, we are not free to say whatever we feel like saying. The reason for a limitation on our speech is because it is such a powerful weapon. In the book of James, the power of the tongue is compared to a bridle in a horse's mouth, the rudder of a ship, and a spark that ignites a forest fire. Every species of animal can be tamed, but it is impossible to tame the tongue. In case we miss the point of all these analogies, James simply said, the tongue is "a restless evil full of deadly poison."

Since speech is such a powerful tool, we are limited in how it can be used. The most basic guideline is that our speech is to be truthful. Therefore, laying aside falsehood, speak truth each one of you with his neighbor, for we are members of one another (Ephesians 4:25). However, even before speaking the truth we should pause to make sure we have heard correctly. This you know, my beloved brethren. But everyone must be quick to hear, slow to speak and slow to anger... (James 1:19). My father frequently reminded me that God gave me two ears and one mouth for a reason. Just because we have something to say does not mean it should be said. I have learned that those who speak the least frequently often have the most valuable things to say.

When it comes to speaking, truth is not the only criteria. We are to speak the truth in love (Ephesians 4:15). Just because something is true does not mean that it should be said. If we cannot say it in love, then we should be silent. This is a difficult task today because of the ability to say random, anonymous things to anyone in the world at any time of the day via the Internet. We are tempted to say things we would never speak if we had to do so face to face.

We still have not exhausted the limitations to our freedom of speech. Let no unwholesome word proceed from your mouth, but only such a word as is good for edification according to the need of the moment, so that it will give grace to those who hear (Ephesians 4:29). The term "unwholesome" means rotten or corrupt. It is derived from a word that is often translated as "evil" and reminds us not to speak words that are designed to harm others. In contrast to this kind of talk, we are encouraged to speak in a much healthier manner: Let your speech always be with grace, as though seasoned with salt, so that you will know how you should respond to each person (Colossians 4:6).

I must confess, I would have fewer things to say if I limited myself to only speaking with grace. But Jesus did warn us about the seriousness of this matter when He said, But I tell you that every careless word that people speak, they shall give an accounting for it in the day of judgment (Matthew 12:36). I don't know about you, but I should probably sort through my Twitter feeds and Facebook posts to see if there is much grace being spoken.

I understand when Americans get all excited about any threat to their freedom of speech. Like everyone else, I certainly want to live in a country where my speech is not limited by political power. I want to be able to discuss and debate issues without fear of punishment. As American citizens, we must be vigilant in maintaining this freedom.

Yet, as a Christian, my first allegiance is to another authority, one who does not grant us freedom of speech. As difficult as it would be to live in a country without freedom, it would be even more damaging to not live in God's kingdom. The First Amendment allows me to say many things that God restricts. If I am to stand up for my rights, I must do so in a way that considers the impact my manner and method of standing has upon others. We are indeed free to voice our support or displeasure with something or someone, but we are not free to say and do hurtful things or to say things that do not bring grace into the situation.

Before we stand up for our freedom of speech, perhaps we should first utter this prayer - Let the words of my mouth and the meditation of my heart be acceptable in Your sight, O LORD, my rock and my Redeemer (Psalms 19:14).

Another area where the modern American church has allowed patriotism to supersede following Christ is with the heavy emphasis on the Second Amendment. If you did a survey among Americans who claim to be Christians, I'm confident more of them could identify the Second Amendment than could identify Jesus' Second Commandment.

What, you didn't realize Jesus had a list of commandments?

Jesus was quite persistent in resisting those who would make Him a legalist. They brought a woman to Him, directly from an adulterous bed, hoping to make Him choose legalism and obey the law. When asked why He allowed His disciples to harvest grain on the Sabbath, He moved beyond the reading of the law to the meaning of the law. After being called out for not washing His hands before a meal according to the rule of law, Jesus reminded His host that cleanliness comes from the heart, not from the wash basin.

Finally, Jesus was cornered by a lawyer. If you want to find a true legalist, look for the nearest lawyer—that is what they do. The lawyer asked Jesus to identify the highest law of Moses. He wanted to know what Jesus thought was the most important law.

Since this man was an expert on the law, he already had an opinion on this issue. He was either expecting Jesus to confirm his own opinion or to offer an opposing position that they could argue.

Jesus provided an answer that would be quite agreeable to the lawyer—love God with all your being. But He didn't stop there, saying there is a second commandment of equal value. The second commandment is to "love your neighbor as yourself" (Matthew 22:39).

That's tough!

I think it means when my neighbor is hungry I should be just as diligent in feeding him as I am in feeding myself when I'm hungry.

I think it means when my neighbor is cold I should make every effort to keep him as warm as I do myself on a winter night.

I think it means when my neighbor is hurting because of a loss (a death, injury, or relationship) I should sit down and grieve with him.

I think it means when my neighbor has screwed up something I should be helping to make things right just like I want others to help me make things right.

I think it means when my neighbor is mean and angry I should forgive him just like I want to be forgiven.

I think it means when my neighbor has stupid opinions I should be gentle and understanding like I need others to treat me when I have stupid opinions.

I think it means I want the best for my neighbor just like I want the best for myself.

Jesus' second commandment is a hard one, but it makes His first commandment visible. In other words, how does anyone know if I actually love God? I can tell you that I do, but I might be lying, perhaps even lying to myself. But in tying these two commandments together, Jesus gave us a way to show that we genuinely love God by revealing how much we love our neighbor.

Do you understand what that means? It means I cannot claim to love God unless I love my neighbor. If I don't care about my neighbor's hunger, or his lack of clothing, or his hurting, or his need for help and forgiveness, then I don't really love God.

Jesus' Second Commandment might be one of the most important things He said.

It is sad that so many will wrap themselves in the protection of the Second Amendment yet fail to comprehend the Second Commandment. If you read them carefully, they are almost opposite in meaning.

The Second Amendment is designed to allow me to protect myself, while the Second Commandment is designed to allow me to give myself to others.

The Second Amendment gives me license to kill someone who wants to steal my stuff, and the Second Commandment gives me license to give my stuff to anyone who needs it.

The Second Amendment focuses on my need to take care of myself (and my family), but the Second Commandment focuses my attention on the needs of others.

It causes me to wonder what would happen if Christians (just those who follow Jesus) were as adamant about demanding their Second Commandment rights as they are about the Second Amendment rights. Perhaps we would stop hating and killing one another and start loving and taking care of one another. Or more importantly, at least for me anyway, what would it mean if I took Jesus' Second Commandment more seriously? How would that change my life? Perhaps it's time to find out.

What is a person to do when two things of great value are in opposition to one another? When our patriotism as an American citizen advocates a particular action and our position as a believer in Christ points in a different direction, what are we to do? That is what happened several years ago on a Sunday evening when the news was broadcast that longtime enemy of America, Osama bin Laden had been killed by American forces.

The first, perhaps spontaneous response from most of us was to rejoice. This was a day that American citizens craved for nearly a decade. This man, one that many would classify as one of the most wicked who has ever lived, was responsible for the death of thousands of Americans. He has caused the entire nation to alter the way we travel and how we gather in large groups. It is hard to imagine that any American would not be elated by the news of this death.

However, many of us are not only Americans; we are also Christians, followers of Jesus. It is hard to imagine Jesus rejoicing in the death of anyone, even one considered as a very evil man. Jesus' world was filled with evil, malicious men. Babies were slaughtered in Bethlehem in the years after his birth; his beloved friend John was senselessly beheaded; Jewish leaders ruthlessly pursued Jesus own death, yet He never advocated retaliation. He specifically cast aside the approach of "an eye for an eye," instead calling His followers to "turn the other cheek." I think it is safe to say that Jesus would not have been among the crowd cheering outside the gates of the White House at the death of America's enemy.

So, what is a Christian American (or, American Christian) to do? Perhaps the most common response is to point to Jesus' words in Mark 12:17 that we should give to Caesar that which is his and to God that which belongs to Him. Some might use these words of Jesus to say that there are times when it is appropriate to be an American and other times when it is not. But I don't think these familiar words of Jesus apply to this situation. Within the original context, Jesus was not speaking of two things that were in opposition to one another, He was addressing the usage of money. It was not an issue of paying taxes or paying a tithe, there is no conflict between faith and being a taxpayer. Doing both is possible.

Sharon and I were watching TV that Sunday night when the announcement came on that the President was going to address the nation in ten minutes. It is unusual in this day of instant communication that we need to wait ten minutes for any kind of news. It reminded me of many years ago when people would gather in front of the television or radio and wait for the President to speak to the nation. I recalled those nervous hours gathered in the living room with my family many many years ago as we waited for news about the Cuban missile crisis. Once again, it did not seem like we were going to hear good news.

I immediately switched to an all-news network, hoping to get an early report about what the President was going to say. It has been a long time since the President spoke to the nation and we did not know beforehand what he was going to say. However, all they were saying was that it was a matter of national security. I would have to wait for ten minutes - then twenty minutes, and thirty, and ultimately more than an hour later.

When I finally heard the news that this terrorist had been killed, my initial reaction was relief. No missile crisis or terrorist threat to worry about! I admit to rejoicing in the situation, but I can honestly say that I did not rejoice in the death of an individual. I didn't give it much thought.

I did think it odd to see people celebrating in the streets, especially a great number of young people who probably have very vague memories of the 9-11 attacks.

But, since I am striving to be honest, I will say that I did not lose any sleep over the death of this wicked, evil, hate-filled man. Perhaps I should have. Numerous Christian writers are trying to make me feel guilty for feeling that this man deserved to die, but I'm sorry, I don't. I know that God loves all people and that Jesus asked for His executioners to be forgiven, which is a standard beyond my ability. Although it is not appropriate to rejoice in the death of anyone, it is certainly fine to breathe a sigh of relief that this terrible threat is gone. If you can reconcile those two thoughts, you are much smarter than me.

While it is true that God loves all, He is the One who sentences all to die (see Romans 6:23). Sin brings about death, and it is often true that those who are the vilest sinners experience the cruelest deaths. That is called justice.

Justice does not always occur in this life, and we should all be thankful for that. But, when it does, that is not a bad thing. Some have suggested that it would have been better if Osama had been taken alive and given a trial in order to satisfy justice. However, he has essentially had a ten-year trial, pled guilty on numerous occasions, and received the death penalty at the hands of the state. Justice was accomplished.

What he did not receive was mercy and that is the work of God. Osama was not sentenced to eternal damnation by the American military, that is the task of a higher authority. Perhaps that is what I should be saddened by. Like most Americans, I can't help but rejoice in the removal of this significant threat to our lives. Whether or not he experiences mercy is not mine to know, but I do trust God to do the right thing.

The American church has become entangled with patriotism. In fact, we might even say that it has become a religion that competes with Christianity for the hearts and minds of people. In the American church...

- God = Freedom
- Scripture = The Constitution
- Salvation = The Republican Party
- The worship experience includes...
  Call to Worship = Declaration of Independence
  Statement of Faith = Pledge of Allegiance
- Worship hymns include...
  God Bless America
  Star Spangled Banner
  America the Beautiful
  Or, if you prefer more contemporary
  Born in the USA
  God Bless the USA
- Holy days celebrated are...

Fourth of July
Memorial Day
Labor Day
Flag Day
President's Day

I have come to the conclusion that many of our churches have become more American than they are Christian. They continue to preach the basic tenants of the faith, but if it comes down to choosing between Christ and the country, they tend to choose country. Many are more willing to fight for their rights as Americans than they are to give up their rights for the sake of Christ.

This has been a significant factor in my choosing to quit going to church. I grew weary of hearing the preacher extol the virtues of his political party and pander to a political platform that had little regard for Jesus' admonitions. When Christians are expected to support and vote for politicians who openly flaunt their immorality merely because they hold certain political ideologies, then the church has given up its prophetic voice.

I understand that people have different political opinions. It is indeed reasonable that we don't all agree on how the government should operate. It makes perfect sense that people understand foreign policy in different ways. There is nothing wrong with disagreeing over what is best for the nation's economy. It is not even expected that all of us should agree on the correct decision on every moral issue. Even among Christians.

To be honest, in the grand scheme of things, there are few absolutes that should be expected of all Christians. Let me try to name them:

- God created
- Jesus is the Son of God
- Jesus is Lord
- Loving one another is imperative
- All of these things should make a difference in the way we live

I'm going to go out on a limb and say that if you claim to be a Christian, then you have given your assent to each of these statements.

We don't have to agree on God's method of creation, nor all the theological gymnastics for debating Jesus' role as God's Son, nor what is the first step in making Jesus Lord of our life, nor what is the best way to demonstrate our love for others. There is room for much diversity among Jesus' followers. I think a reading of the New Testament will provide evidence to this truth.

Matthew was a tax-collector, a Jew who had sold out to the Romans. Simon was called a Zealot, a political party that advocated overthrowing the Romans. Paul was an ardent persecutor of the church who became the most famous missionary for the church. Thomas doubted the reality before his eyes.

Paul's writings are heavy on Jesus' fulfillment of the law. John's writings emphasize God's great love and grace. The Book of James was almost excluded from the Bible because of its legalism.

There is great variety among the followers of Jesus.

Yet, despite all our differences, there are some values that have been shared by the vast majority of Christians throughout history. I will try to enumerate those values:

- Honesty
- Sexual morality (although definitions change over time, it is still safe to assume Christians do not approve of things like infidelity, rape, incest, and sexual violence)
- Peacefulness
- Kindness (such as basic good manners)
- Non-violence (not speaking about nations going to war, but about one person physically hurting or taking advantage of another person)

I feel safe in saying that historically, Christians have encouraged honesty, sexual morality, peace, kindness, and non-violence. Therefore, we can say that Christians have taken a stand against dishonesty, sexual immorality, chaos, meanness, and violence.

I'm not naive; I'm aware that there have been many professed Christians, often acting in the name of Christ, who have been liars, cheaters, and violence practitioners. However, the church as a whole has stood against these things. Christians typically turn away from these people and frequently take a public stand that these behaviors are not acceptable.

Things have certainly changed. Surveys indicate that evangelical Christians (in the past the ones most demanding of the above qualities) overwhelming support political candidates we never would have supported in the past. If I remember correctly, Christians were appalled when Bill Clinton was guilty of immoral behavior in the White House. We knew what "is" "was" and we didn't like it.

Today we have politicians who grope women, body slam reporters, threaten to shoot fellow politicians in the head, tell obvious lies, use their position to enhance their bank accounts, publicly call people unkind names, and many other unseemly behaviors. All the while, Christians take to Facebook and Twitter to offer explanations, excuses, and continued support. I don't get it.

Although he's not the only politician that fits the category but let's be honest, we all know I'm speaking of President Trump. If it were not for evangelical Christians, he would still be slumming around New York living in Trump Tower instead of flying around the world on Air Force One.

I don't want to hear that nonsense that at least he's better than Hillary. She has been out of the picture since the election was over, so you can't blame her any longer.

She is not running for office, so it doesn't matter if his opponent was worse (I have repeatedly said neither candidate was a good choice). Now the question becomes, why do Christians still support this man? How do you justify speaking up for someone who is so contrary to what we have always claimed were traditional Christian values?

Robert Jeffress, the pastor of what was one of the leading churches in the country at one time, has defended the President by claiming that his affair with an adult film star is irrelevant because to support him is not to compromise our beliefs because the President is displaying strong leadership and promoting the right political agenda.

If you take the position that you support his policies, then you are essentially saying that political policy takes precedence over Christian values. If you take the position that you want a businessman to strengthen our economy, then you are essentially saying that you value money more than character. If you like his motto of America First, then you are saying the country comes before Christ.

Tell me how a Christian can support a man who has lived his entire life in opposition to the things Christians have held onto as core values—values like honesty, sexual morality, peacefulness, kindness, and non-violence.

The argument that all politicians have the same problem is only correct because Christians have allowed it to happen. If we had consistently stood for people with the proper values, then we would find them among our choices. However, once we abdicated the standards, there is no reason that people who live according to these standards should run for office because Christians won't necessarily vote for them. If it is true that people with values will not enter politics, then it is because Christians have not supported them in the past. It is our fault.

We are getting what we wanted.

But none of this is new since our current President came along. Several years ago, I was in a hospital waiting room as my father was in surgery. As you probably know, there's not much to do on such occasions but to visit with others in the room. One such person was a man who was a friend of my Dad. He was a nice, friendly man and enjoyable to converse with.

However, he kept getting off on the subject of politics. He knew Daddy was a retired preacher and that I had been actively working for churches, so he also felt comfortable talking about church matters. He frequently mentioned how disgusted he was with the current Democrat President and how supportive his church was of Republican policies and politicians. I didn't say much because it wasn't time for a political argument.

He finally suggested that I should visit his church, thinking I would enjoy their great fellowship. He looked somewhat puzzled when I asked if they had a special class for Democrats. When he questioned what I meant,

Why I Quit Going to Church

I just asked if it was necessary to be a Republican to attend his church.

Obviously, there's not a written rule enforcing that requirement for any church, but I have been in many where if you're not a supporter of a particular political issue then you will not feel welcome. Pastors use sermons to pound home the necessity to support political positions. Politicians are invited to share the pulpit on Sunday morning to advocate for their agenda. Comments made in the foyer and in small group sessions suggest the stupidity of holding the wrong political position.

One Sunday afternoon we visited my mother in her assisted living apartment. She was headed out for church service, so we invited ourselves to go along. When we arrived at the gathering, folks were excited to see us "young people." I was appreciative of the three or four people who came from a local church to sing and encourage and preach.

However, as the service time was winding down, the man who preached asked for special prayer for our nation, especially our President who needed to be saved.

I almost lost control at that point. Barak Obama was our President at the time, and I don't recall having another President who spoke so eloquently of his Christian faith and lived it out in his personal life. To listen to someone suggest he needed to "be saved" because he didn't agree with his political positions was more than I could handle.

I didn't cause a scene (my mother and my wife would have strangled me), but I did say to the preacher as he shook my hand on the way out that I didn't appreciate his political reference and he needed to keep politics out of his sermon. He was there to minister to old folks who needed comfort for the every day struggles faced by people nearing the end. This preacher was more interested in scoring points with the team members who were with him than actually serving the people he came to serve.

That Sunday afternoon experience sums up much of what is happening in churches all over the country every Sunday. Rather than loving and caring for those who need the presence of Christ in their lives, the church is putting together a rally designed to win elections. The church has become little more than a Republican Party caucus.

Critical and Judgmental

The Pharisees of Jesus' day have taken a lot of grief over the past two millennia. We think of them as sour-faced, straight-laced, fundamentalist preachers whose sole purpose was to make everyone else as miserable as them. They were the ones who came up with the "No Mixed Bathing" rules that were enforced at Christian summer camps. We have also credited them with the point system printed on offering envelopes that we filled out as kids – 20 for attendance, 20 for offering brought, 20 for studying the lesson, 20 for bringing a guest, and 20 for reading our Bible – or something like that. They probably put a stop to a lot of dances in their day as well.

When we were kids, my sister would frequently earn one of those lapel pins for attending Sunday School every week for a year. I never made it all fifty-two weeks. Either a bad cold or stomach virus hindered my best efforts. On vacation, my mother never let us cheat. Other kids expected to be excused because they were out of town. We had to visit a church wherever we were, or it didn't count. I always pictured the Pharisees as having a long train of attendance pins, stretching from their lapel to the ground.

When people today speak of Pharisees it is likely they are equated with the leaders of the church. It is common to hear them speak of the church being pharisaical when being judgmental or critical. When they want to criticize the church, reference is usually made to the way Jesus spoke to the Pharisees – "He condemned the Pharisees just like he would accuse the church leaders today." It is common to hear the claim that if Jesus were present today, he would criticize church leaders just as He did the Pharisees of His time.

One of the main problems with the Pharisees of Jesus' day was their critical, judgmental spirit. They felt like they were defenders of the truth and anyone who didn't follow their teaching deserved condemnation. One of their favorite subjects was Sabbath observance. They were especially critical of Jesus and his failure to live according to the restrictions they felt were necessary.

Just like Jesus' day, there is a judgmental attitude toward anyone who is considered a sinner. However, one of the problems is that our definition of sin keeps changing over time. When I was a kid, divorce was a big deal for many Christians. People who had been divorced often spoke of as being treated as failures and outcasts by the church. They were excluded from positions of leadership, especially from staff positions. There was a real stigma because divorce was considered a grave sin.

Malachi 2:16 says that God hates divorce, so it was understood that God's people should also hate divorce. The problem is that the church took that simple statement too far. If you have ever had a loved one (or perhaps yourself) experience a divorce, it can cause you to rethink that position. For too long we read that statement to mean that God hates divorced people. That is not what it says. He hates divorce.

The reason God hates divorce is because it is painful, destructive, and damaging to everyone involved. If your heart has been broken as you stood helplessly as your child got divorced, imagine how much more God feels when those He loves suffer. Divorce is undoubtedly something to be hated. However, divorced people need grace and mercy to see them through the difficult time.

For the most part, the church has moved away from this position on marriage and divorce. Yet, other "sins" have come to the forefront. This list of "sins" has included things like drinking alcohol, misusing drugs, lying and cheating, among others. Today, the list of sins would undeniably include homosexuality and all gender questioning attitudes and activities (there's got to be a better way to explain this without writing an entire book). Abortion is another that is at the forefront of the church's thinking today.

The purpose of this chapter is not to come to the defense of sinners, or to argue about whether or not these are sins, but to discuss the attitude of the church toward these folks. One of the most obvious ways we have missed the teaching of Jesus is the way we relate to sinners. Our approach has typically been more akin to the Pharisees than to Jesus.

The New Testament Pharisees were good at excluding anyone who did not live as they should. They often went so far as to avoid all physical contact with these "unclean" people for fear such contact would make them unclean as well. It makes you wonder if they had those bulky hazmat suits back in the first century if the Pharisees would have worn them for religious reasons.

People today stay away from the church for the same reasons people in Jesus' day avoided the Pharisees. They don't want to be judged, criticized, and condemned. Like the Pharisees, the church is not even aware it is happening. Churches today believe they are merely standing up for what is right, that they are fighting for God.

However, put yourself in the position of someone who has been labeled by the church as a sinner. If you were a young woman who had an abortion, would you feel comfortable in church? Or if you were attracted to people of the same sex, or wrestling about being comfortable with your own birth sex, do you think you would be a welcome addition to your neighborhood congregation?

Even something as silly as political opinions can cause you to feel unclean or unworthy by many churches. When the pastor stands in the pulpit and espouses a specific political opinion while the congregation nods in assent, anyone who supports a different political position would definitely feel unwelcome. This is what happens when the church takes on the task of political persuasion.

One of the most blatant examples of this type of religious judgmentalism is seen in the actions of Westboro Baptist Church in Kansas. This congregation is notorious in condemning anyone even remotely connected to something they define as homosexual. They even protest at fallen soldier's funerals because in fighting for our country they were supporting a nation that doesn't ban homosexuality.

I'm not suggesting that other churches are like Westboro. In fact, as far as I know, this small congregation stands alone in their extreme position. However, just because the church hasn't become extreme doesn't mean it has not become judgmental.

Let me hasten to add that this judgmental attitude toward others is not a problem confined to conservative churches. It was many years ago that I first heard the saying, "Christians are the only army that shoots its own wounded." I am confident the statement is much older than me since I suspect Christians have been known to do this to one another for a long time. It is not a new pastime, but the practice has certainly been fine-tuned in our world today.

Think back a couple of years ago to the revelation that one of the Duggar children had molested young girls when he was a teenager. You remember the Duggar family; the family with 19 children who have been featured on one of those television "reality" (are you kidding) shows. If you believe those shows are representative of reality, I would like to speak to you about some investment opportunities.

When the world found out that Josh Duggar, the oldest of the 19, was guilty of inappropriate behavior with several girls when he was a teenager himself a dozen years ago, folks went crazy and lit up the social media circuit. It appears that neither his parents nor the authorities handled things appropriately when he confessed his actions. All of us would like to have seen harsher penalties or stricter punishment, or at least that is what we pontificate, even though we know very little about the situation and the people involved.

But here is the thing that bothers me. It seems that every Christian with a blog jumped into the fray, and many of them imply that Josh Duggar (and his father, and his mother, and his uncle, and the television network, and the Arkansas police, and everyone who has ever watched the show) is one of the worst sinners since Bill Clinton and Monica Lewinsky.

It seems that the actions of this teenage boy have nullified everything many people have stood for over the years. If you are pro-life—what an idiot you are; look at what this pro-lifer did! If you have opposed gay marriage—don't you feel stupid now that one of yours has proven to be immoral! If you thought it was fine for people to strive to live a family life that is centered on God's Word—now you know that's a stupid idea. If you have conservative values—it is time for you to move on and get a life since one of your own messed up! God forbid that you homeschooled your children—you should probably be put away as a menace to society.

By the way, if you don't understand sarcasm, please disregard the previous paragraph.

A young boy sexually assaulting young girls is a sin, but it is not the unpardonable sin, nor does it nullify everything that he has believed or said for his entire life. There should have been (and possibly still should be) appropriate punishment. Proper counseling and prayer should also be available to his victims—something we can all do.

There are lessons to be learned from this situation; hopefully, lessons that can lessen the chances of this happening again, although we have not been very successful in other areas when we have tried to eliminate sin.

A while back, the pastor of a large church in a neighboring city showed up on national television excoriating the President for not being the kind of Christian he thinks he should be.

Don't misunderstand. I think it is appropriate to disagree with policies and platforms and vigorously and aggressively make your case. I also think it is fitting to speak out against immorality and sinful behavior of politicians (although it should probably be done with the same tenderness and love that you would express to someone listening to one of your sermons).

But, when a Christian leader shows up on television to provide a smug, smarmy, sarcastic diatribe, claiming to speak for "evangelical Christians" because the President failed to issue an official proclamation about Easter, I can't help but be embarrassed. I am not easily embarrassed. I grew up with a lot of physical malfunctions, so my body has been poked, prodded, and handled by doctors, nurses, and airport security personnel all of my life. I spent several years working in a police department, so I have heard and seen people at their worst. I am not overly absorbed with what other people think and say about me. As I said, I am not easily embarrassed.

It is only possible to be embarrassed when you care about losing something. It is the things that are most important to us that cause humiliation. I am embarrassed when my children do something stupid, but when your children act up I am just angry. I might be embarrassed by getting a traffic ticket, but I might chuckle as a drive past you talking to a traffic officer on the shoulder of the highway.

Yet, I am now confessing that I am frequently embarrassed. To be more specific, I am embarrassed to be known as a Christian. Let me clarify before I move on. I am not embarrassed by anything that Jesus has done or that He has asked me to do. Obviously, I am disappointed and saddened that I have not been quick to obey many times. But the source of my embarrassment is the way many of my Christian brothers and sisters have conducted themselves.

With each pollical election cycle, the vitriol gets worse, but it seems worse when Christians are leading the charge. My email inbox gets filled with charges of liar, fraud, terrorist, and anti-Christ against every public figure. Christian blogs prophesied that an incorrect vote would turn our nation in Sodom and Gomorrah.

I understand hyperbole and the use of metaphor in political debate. This was much more. Many Christians were motivated by anger and hate. Racism and rage were commonly heard in the voices of some of our Christian leaders. It is embarrassing that as followers of Jesus we have resorted to name-calling, lies, innuendo, and false accusations when it comes to political debate. We can–we must–do better!

Since I am only responsible for my actions and attitudes, I will begin the process of doing better in my own life. I will first seek God's forgiveness for my own anger and for my silence when I should have stood in defense of those who were being abused.

Secondly, I will accept the truth that God is responsible for the winners of our elections, at least that is the way I read the words of the Apostle Paul - Let every person be in subjection to the governing authorities. For there is no authority except from God, and those which exist are established by God. (Romans 13:1) These words were originally written to a community that had a much more difficult political climate than you or I have ever experienced. The early readers probably had friends and family members who were used as torches to light Nero's garden.

Third, I will try harder to pray for those that God has placed in a position of authority. In fact, other than being required by Jesus to pay my taxes, this seems to be the only requirement I have as a Christian citizen—"I urge, then, first of all, that requests, prayers, intercession and thanksgiving be made for everyone—for kings and all those in authority, that we may live peaceful and quiet lives in all godliness and holiness" (1 Timothy 2:1-2).

Praying for those in authority is a beautiful thing. It's much more difficult to criticize someone we're praying for. It's impossible to spread lies and accusations about someone on your prayer list. Prayer not only benefits the recipient of the prayer, but it cleanses us of anger and hate toward that person.

Being critical and judgmental is not the best approach for Christians and I'll be the first to admit, I've got much to learn. It is certainly not the approach recommended by Jesus when He said, "Judge not lest you be judged" (Matthew 7:1).

At this point, let me add that criticism of immorality is fair game. It is important for Christians to stand against depraved behavior. To do so is to stand in line with John the Baptizer who was beheaded for condemning King Herod's immorality. Jesus called John the greatest man who ever lived.

The American church today seems to build around the task of separating the sheep and the goats to make sure the sheep are in the fold, and the goats remain outside the fold. This kind of judgment is not ours to make. When we take the matter into our hands, we have ceased being the church established by Jesus and instead followed the path of the Pharisees.

American Christianity and Dementia

During the past couple of years, my family has walked the arduous journey of Dementia with my mother. She has moved rapidly from a healthy alert woman living by herself, to a senior living environment, to assisted living, to memory care, and now to nursing care. Perhaps the thing that is most difficult about the process is knowing that improvement is not going to happen.

I have often wondered what it must be like not knowing who you are or where you are. Forgetting your past and even your identity makes you do things that are entirely out of character. A couple of times Mama has slapped one of her caregivers and even used inappropriate language. These things are completely unlike who she is and has been her entire life. Most of the time her caregivers speak about her kindness and sweet personality, but those ugly responses have appeared a few times.

I bring this up because Dementia seems to be an accurate metaphor for the American church. It seems as if the church is experiencing a similar debilitating disease, forgetting who it is and what it's supposed to be. Let me remind you that I'm not referring to the church identified in the Bible as the body of Christ. I'm speaking of the American church—the church that embraced the notion that being a follower of Christ is equivalent to being an American.

It came on almost imperceptibly. For several years, Daddy talked about Mama losing her memory, but since none of us were with her every day we thought he was exaggerating. After he died, and we were more involved with her life, it was noticeable she was struggling.

In like fashion, almost imperceptibility, the American church began to lose its identity and history. I'm certainly not qualified to write a history of the American church, but I can offer one example that suggests this might be the case—the issue of abortion.

It wasn't that long ago, at least in my lifetime, evangelical Christians were not as singularly focused on the issue of abortion. The Roe v. Wade Supreme Court Decision allowing abortions was issued in 1973. Addressing that decision, W.A. Criswell, pastor of First Baptist Church, Dallas, Texas, spoke out in support of the ruling with these words: "I have always felt that it was only after a child was born and had a life separate from its mother that it became an individual person," he said, "and it has always, therefore, seemed to me that what is best for the mother and for the future should be allowed."

In fact, two years earlier, the Southern Baptist Convention passed a resolution encouraging "Southern Baptists to work for legislation that will allow the possibility of abortion under such conditions as rape, incest, clear evidence of severe fetal deformity, and carefully ascertained evidence of the likelihood of damage to the emotional, mental, and physical health of the mother."

Indeed, times have changed, and now the predominate American church position is that all abortions are wrong, and for some extremists, even in the case of the mother's potential death. It has become expected that Christians will oppose abortion at any cost.

The point of all of this is not to make the case that abortion should be allowed or that it should not be limited. I agree that abortion is wrong and would never advocate for any abortion except under extreme circumstances. The overwhelming majority of abortions are wrong and not healthy for the moral condition of our society.

What has happened is that the American church has moved from the pre-Roe v. Wade position when abortion was frowned upon but not the make-or-break test of faith that it has become today. Because it has become such a crucial issue for the American church, it makes every action to eliminate abortion acceptable. We see this with some who have even approved of killing abortion doctors.

The American church has adopted similarly strong feelings to other issues, most notably homosexuality and gun ownership. Consequently, the primary task of the church is no longer understood as making disciples of Jesus, but of making adherents of these political positions. Such a change in the American church didn't happen overnight. It has taken decades. It was gradual, almost imperceptible at times, but now here we are.

We have leaders of the American church, empowered by a loyal band of followers, who ignore moral failures of politicians as long as they will help eliminate abortions, condemn homosexuality, and fight for gun rights. Pastors invite politicians to stand in their pulpits and recruit voters and volunteers.

Like my mother forgetting who she is, the American church has forgotten the church existed long before America existed, and if God chooses, will exist long after America is gone. It's time to lay aside the political positions that shape the American church and take up the teachings of Jesus—they are not the same. Jesus said nothing about abortion, homosexuality, or gun ownership.

The American church must gather around the cross, not the American flag. The American church must get off the Republican bandwagon and follow the narrow road of Jesus. The American church must relearn the value of helping the lame, blind, and poor. The American church must put its hope in God, not in a man-made constitution.

There is no cure for Dementia, and I recently learned its one of the leading causes of death in this country. To be honest, I don't have much hope for a cure of the American church either. Once you have forgotten your identity and values, there's little hope of returning to health and viability.

One Saturday evening I was preparing for a Pentecost Sunday service for our little group and I thought it would be good to spend our time together focusing on the work of the Holy Spirit. The music, activities, Scripture reading, and study were all built around the work of God's Spirit in our lives. As I prepared for my part of the evening, it dawned on me that our little group has a religious background that is more varied than a giant bag of M&M's. It was clear we would be approaching this subject from different viewpoints, which caused me a little apprehension.

Hoping to diffuse any potential disagreement that can often arise when people have different opinions about an important subject, I choose to be proactive and try to head off any controversy. At the outset I affirmed our diversity. To illustrate the point, I asked several to share the various Christian traditions in their background. I was aware of our diversity, but to listen to folks list their experiences really put things in perspective. I can't remember them all, but these are some of the terms we heard

– Baptist (including moderate, conservative, missionary, and fundamental), Catholic, Jewish, Methodist, Charismatic, Lutheran, Atheist, Mormon, and Nigerian Baptist.

At that point it was apparent we needed to disband our little fellowship and go our separate ways!

Not really. No one was surprised because we have been an extremely diverse group from the beginning. Yet, it works. We get along. Once we shared our variety of backgrounds, I pointed out the obvious. Everyone is accepted in our little group. We do not have a background check or test of your orthodoxy before you can participate. If you are present, then you belong.

However, it is equally important that we realize not only are we accepted, but another great blessing is that we have the opportunity to learn from others who are different from us. I read the Bible and life through the lens of someone who was raised and educated as a conservative Baptist. That does not mean I simply recite conservative Baptist doctrine. But it does mean my background and experience shade my current doctrine.

My friend John, who was also there Sunday evening, has a different lens with a plethora of reflections. He was raised in a Missionary Baptist church, studied to be a Catholic priest, has experience in the Jewish faith, as well as a charismatic church. He can teach me a lot (and he has) if I listen. I suspect he can also learn a few things from me. John and I have other differences that are significant. For example, he's African American and I'm not - even my hair is mostly white.

Mary, who led us through the activity for the evening, has a Ph.D. from a Jesuit university, was Mormon years ago, has some Baptist in her from a time of living in the Texas panhandle, and who knows what else. She has an even different lens on life.

Recently, I was asked to complete a questionnaire about our church. They wanted to know about our "Target Audience." I struggled with that question because we don't really have one. Among our group of about 30 who are in and out of our fellowship, our age range is from 80's to preteens. We are ethnically diverse, economically diverse, educationally diverse, and as we have already seen, theologically diverse. It sounds too grandiose to say the whole world is our target audience. But, we truly mean it when we say all are welcome.

How big is your church? When you gather on Sunday are you surrounded by people just like you? Could your church have a discussion about the Holy Spirit without being polarized? Or dogmatic?

Many churches have a "Target Audience" and try to gather folks together who are much like one another. It might make it easier to build an audience because you all like to see and do the same things and struggle with the same needs. When that happens, you are missing out on a richness that only occurs when a ragtag group of people gathers around the Lord Jesus. That is precisely what happened when Jesus singled out his first group of followers – a tax-collector, a political zealot, several fishermen, brothers, and strangers. In fact, our little group is even more diverse – we are not all Jewish men.

Jesus appeals to every type of person. If we are not attracting every type of person to our church, it might suggest Jesus is not the drawing card.

The Christian faith has always been, at least since the time of the founder Jesus, the place of taking care of the suffering, outcast, poor, and despised. One of my favorite stories, since I was first taught it over and over as a child, is Jesus' story of the Good Samaritan.

In case you don't recall, it goes like this. A man was beaten, robbed, and left to die on a dangerous, desolate road. The first two to pass by were religious leaders, but they continued on as if they did not see the man. Perhaps they ignored him because they didn't care, but more likely out of fear, because it was a trail on the wrong side of the tracks.

A third man, identified as a Samaritan, came by. It was an important detail since the Samaritans were despised in Jesus' day. Perhaps today we would call him a Muslim or a Syrian or an African-American, whatever your prejudice might be. This man took the risk, bandaged the wounds, loaded the man up, and took him to the hospital.

The point of Jesus' tale is that He expects His followers to be like the Samaritan. It is expected that we should risk our safety, our possessions, our security when we encounter someone in need. Jesus said final judgment would not be based on whether we recited the "Sinner's Prayer," but based on our care and concern for those who have been beaten and bruised by the world (see Matthew 25).

Yet, as we are experiencing today, massive numbers of Christians, out of fear, have been tempted to flee the Christian faith that is characterized by these words of Jesus. It is the temptation to become a refugee from the Christian faith. When we are afraid our own safety will be jeopardized by reaching out in compassion to those in need, then we are refugees from the faith of Jesus. Like the first two travelers in Jesus' story of the Samaritan, concern for our own safety has caused us to adopt a new home, one that is not the Christian faith.

The possibility of losing security is not the only fear that can cause us to become Christian refugees. There is also a fear of losing our lifestyle. Like many of you, I'm comfortable where I live, and with all the stuff I have accumulated to make this life possible. I am tempted to do whatever is necessary in order to keep it all safe, even if it means not taking care of the poor. When we get to the point of not being able to give generously, even if we have wealth, we have become refugees from the Christian faith. It is best noticed in those who can't afford to give freely to those in need because they have to make their house/car/boat payments.

This idea comes across in our political positions when we are more concerned with keeping our taxes low than in providing for the poor. When we are more worried about the money in our pocket or the balance in our checking account than we are about those with no money in their pockets and no checking account, then we have left the faith. We are truly Christian refugees—those leaving their home out of fear. When we live in fear of losing our lifestyle, we are not walking the path Jesus called us to walk (see 1 Timothy 6:10).

I also see a third fear, and that is the fear of losing our rights. It has always been perplexing to hear Christians talk about having "rights." That is a concept that seems foreign to the New Testament. The only incident that comes to mind of a believer having rights is the Apostle Paul appealing to his right as a Roman citizen to have an official appeal to Caesar (Acts 25). However, in that case, he did not fight for his right out of fear; he simply utilized a right he already owned as a citizen. He was not fighting to keep his right, but simply utilized his right.

Refugees are driven by fear, which makes it the strangest of ironies for Christians to be afraid. There are numerous reminders in scripture that we should not be afraid. One of the most explicit expressions was made by Jesus Himself (see Matthew 6:24-34). The final remark Jesus made in that passage is that non-believers are the ones who live in fear of not having security or provisions; it is not something that should concern His followers.

There are many Christian refugees—people who have wandered away from the true Christian faith because of fear of losing something valuable to them.

Some will remind me that we are not only Christians, but also, we are Americans. Therefore, we have an obligation to fight for our security, possessions, and rights. People will say they are not leaving the faith; they are merely defending their country, which is founded on their faith.

I don't disagree with that fact that as Americans we have a responsibility to protect our nation, which includes our freedoms and our stuff. However, the problem comes when we place our American citizenship over our Kingdom citizenship. Whenever our responsibility as an American stands in opposition to our Christian faith, it will be evident which one is the most important to us.

Let me illustrate by using the contemporary Syrian refugee issue. Our nation's leaders want to close the doors to refugees from that country. It is built on the fear that they will cause us harm and cost money.

God's word, in particular, the words of Jesus, is unambiguous that we have a responsibility to open our doors to care for those who are in danger. By the way, that is precisely what caused Lot's problems with his neighbors in the city of Sodom—he opened his home to strangers. Thousands of folks are fleeing war, persecution, poverty, and certain death. We have the opportunity to open our homes (borders) for them to find safety. Yet, out of fear, we are tempted to slam the door shut on them.

This is not the place to debate the risk or the vetting process. My point is that as followers of Jesus there is no room for fear being a part of the argument. When we make a decision to turn them away based on fear, then we have wandered away from the faith of Jesus, and we have become refugees ourselves.

Fear is a real thing experienced by all of us in varying degrees. It is capable of plaguing and paralyzing our lives. However, as followers of Jesus, we must never allow fear to cause us to wander away from the faith and become Christian refugees.

I will lift up my eyes to the mountains; From whence shall my help come?

My help comes from the LORD, Who made heaven and earth.

He will not allow your foot to slip; He who keeps you will not slumber.

Behold, He who keeps Israel Will neither slumber nor sleep.

The LORD is your keeper; The LORD is your shade on your right hand.

The sun will not smite you by day, Nor the moon by night.

The LORD will protect you from all evil; He will keep your soul.

The LORD will guard your going out and your coming in From this time forth and forever. (Psalms 121:1-8)

Every Christmas, we gather in our churches and listen to the story, or perhaps see it played out on stage in front of our eyes, of Joseph and Mary on a perilous journey. When we come to the part about them being turned away because there was no room in the inn, if you are like me you will feel a touch of anger within your heart, and perhaps hear yourself say, "I would have let them in." The truth is, we still have the opportunity to allow Jesus into our homes. Remember, it is Jesus who said, "...to the extent that you did it to one of these brothers of Mine, even the least of them, you did it to Me" (Matthew 25:40).

Please be careful and do not allow your concerns as an American citizen take precedence over your obligations as a Kingdom citizen.

Conclusion

I'm sitting at my desk writing this final chapter even though it's a holiday weekend—Memorial Day. It has already been a busy weekend with several family activities and other necessary time consumers. Even though it's Sunday, Sharon and I didn't go to church. We do go occasionally, but not with any regularity.

Yesterday, we talked about getting up and going this week, but it didn't happen. This morning, as I thought about it being Memorial Day Weekend, it occurred to me that if we went, we would probably be confronted with a big patriotic emphasis.

I'm not unpatriotic. In fact, three times this week I sang the National Anthem, listened to "God Bless America" twice, and even recited the Pledge of Allegiance once. Also, I learned that there is actually a Pledge to the

Texas Flag which I didn't know even existed. However, the church is not the place for any of that.

My fear was confirmed when I saw an announcement today, and it was even on the Evening News, that a megachurch in DFW had a guest speaker. Oliver North was introduced by the pastor as a "great American hero." He received a rousing standing ovation and then spoke for twenty-five minutes about the history of Memorial Day and how we should appreciate our soldiers.

I tried to imagine the early church gathering as Paul, or Peter, or one of the other Apostles stood up to address the congregation, and they praised the power of the Roman army. For some reason, I just couldn't get that image in my mind. There's nothing wrong with feeling grateful for the blessings and freedoms we enjoy as American citizens. However, it is not the work of the church to deliver that message.

Oliver North was recently named as the new President of the National Rifle Association, a highly controversial organization. By inviting him to speak politically, not spiritually (I listened to his message), how did that church make those who don't share his politics feel? They were essentially saying "our church supports this political position and you'll probably be uncomfortable here if you don't agree."

This is confirmation of the point of this book—the church has become something it was never intended to be. That's why I quit going to church.

What now? That's a valid question because it's not enough to criticize the church and leave it to die a slow death. Let me hasten to say that I've never had a desire to kill (or even harm) the church. To be honest, Jesus promised that even the gates of Hell will not prevail against it so who am I to think I can cause harm.

In addition, I have never encouraged anyone else to follow my example and leave the church. I simply tell my story along with my reasons and leave the matter between you and God. When our boys were young, we took them out of school and provided homeschooling for them. We did it for reasons that were personal to us and not necessarily applicable to anyone else. Consequently, we did not set out on a crusade to encourage others to leave the schools. I don't recall ever encouraging another parent to homeschool their kid.

The same is true with church. I have reasons for leaving the church which I have documented in this book. These are changes I think need to be made in how church is done, however, I have no idea how that impacts your relationship with the church. I'm not starting a movement; I'm merely describing why I'm part of a movement that has already begun.

I believe the long-term solution will be found with a return to a model of doing church that is much like the early church—specifically home churches. This model proved effective in the first century and has also been successful in many countries since. Meeting in small groups in homes does eliminate several of the problems I describe on the pages of this book.

Sharon and I have made several attempts to host a home church. We have had very little success but plan to continue trying. In the meantime, we are diligent with the spiritual disciplines of prayer, Bible study, ministry, and service to those in need. We pray daily for opportunities to exercise our faith. We occasionally drop in on a neighborhood church, not to criticize but to worship with other believers.

My desire is nothing more than to see Jesus lifted up as the head of the church. I hope and pray that the words on these pages have contributed to that goal.

Terry Austin has always been willing to test boundaries and challenge the status quo. He has written previous books on the church from the perspective of an active church leader. That experience led him to write this book to address critical issues facing the American church today. Terry is a writer and book publisher living in Fort Worth, Texas. All of his writing can be found at www.abpbooks.com.

www.ingramcontent.com/pod-product-compliance
Lightning Source LLC
Chambersburg PA
CBHW051836090426
42736CB00011B/1835